IN
SEARCH
OF
ANCIENT
KINGS

Egúngún in Brazil

IN SEARCH OF ANCIENT KINGS

Egúngún in Brazil

Brian Willson

Foreword by
Robert Farris Thompson

University Press of Mississippi / Jackson

The University Press of Mississippi is the scholarly publishing
agency of the Mississippi Institutions of Higher Learning:
Alcorn State University, Delta State University, Jackson State
University, Mississippi State University, Mississippi University
for Women, Mississippi Valley State University, University of
Mississippi, and University of Southern Mississippi.

www.upress.state.ms.us

The University Press of Mississippi is a member
of the Association of University Presses.

The AfroRomanGaraU and AfroRomanSansU regular, bold,
italic, and bold-italic fonts in this work are available from
https://www.linguistsoftware.com/afrou.htm.

All photographs are courtesy of the author.

First printing 2021
∞

Library of Congress Cataloging-in-Publication Data

Names: Willson, Brian, author. | Thompson, Robert Farris, author of
foreword.
Title: In search of ancient kings : Egúngún in Brazil / Brian Willson ;
foreword by Robert Farris Thompson.
Description: Jackson : University Press of Mississippi, 2021. | Includes
bibliographical references and index.
Identifiers: LCCN 2021015811 (print) | LCCN 2021015812 (ebook) | ISBN
9781496834461 (hardback) | ISBN 9781496834454 (trade paperback) | ISBN
9781496834478 (epub) | ISBN 9781496834485 (epub) | ISBN 9781496834492
(pdf) | ISBN 9781496834508 (pdf)
Subjects: LCSH: Egúngún (Cult)—Brazil. | Yoruba (African
people)—Brazil—Religion.
Classification: LCC BL2592.E38 W55 2021 (print) | LCC BL2592.E38
(ebook)
| DDC 299.6/7—dc23
LC record available at https://lccn.loc.gov/2021015811
LC ebook record available at https://lccn.loc.gov/2021015812

British Library Cataloging-in-Publication Data available

For my parents,
Evelyn Dolores Purdy Willson
and Edgar Arnold Willson
two rays of sun

CONTENTS

Contents

ACKNOWLEDGMENTS

I have many people to thank for their support.

My wife Sonia and family, who tolerated me taking over the dining room for months and months with the walls plastered with Post-its from end to end, and gave me constant support. Thank you to my daughter Katelyn for creating the beautiful charts for the book, and her keen perceptions and insights along with her sharp editing skills. And to my brother and sister Bill and Ev for their constant support, and friends Arnie and Liz Lang.

Thank you to Robert Farris Thompson, from meeting him thirty-five years ago, to hanging out at SOB's, to the numerous lunches and dinners in New Haven these past ten years while I worked on the book. He has continually guided and inspired me, and was a patient interview subject, after I realized these sociable dinners were lost opportunities for retaining his *aşe*-filled words. ("Ask me more, man! What else you got?") Our mutual love of Carlos, his mother Aildés, and Egúngún inspired us to travel deep in our conversations, all reinforced by our shared love of my godmother Betty, whom he knew very well.

To Danny Dawson for the enlightened conversation about origins of Candomblé and ongoing support. Thank you to Lisa Earl Castillo, and Henry Drewal for their knowledge and support. Thank you to Susan Davis of the National Writers Union, a terrific organization, and Awo Fernando Ramirez for his guidance and generosity.

Special thanks to Moussa Kone for creating the beautiful art of the cover. More of his work can be found at orisaimage.com.

Thanks to my spiritual family for support: Babá Adewale Bó-gunmbẹ̀, the *àwíṣẹ* of Idoland, and his never-ending patience with my nonstop questions; and Ìyálóde Ifáṣẹ̀yẹ Ọ̀ṣunwunmi, and Awo Fatoyebi, the two other pillars of the temple Ilé Ọ̀krànràn Onílẹ̀, of which I am member.

Many thanks to my good friend and translator, the wonderful Brazilian actress/dancer/model Viviane Porto and all my Brazilian friends who have helped and supported me: Stefano, who hosted me in his wonderful *pousadas*; Eve D'Amours from Afro-Reggae; the fantastic percussionists Beto Bonfim and Gilberto Gil; my goddaughter Laila Rosa; and Fernando Hashimoto—who first brought me to Brazil.

Muito obrigado to Babá Carlos Ojé Dúdú, one of the most magnificent humans I've ever known, who took me in as family and welcomed me with open arms and open heart after a mere afternoon of food and conversation. And to his wife Cintia, with the indomitable force of Ọya, a remarkable person whose love and affection never fail to move me.

Thank you to my spiritual brothers Fabio and Marlon, who were initiated side by side with me during those nine days—they are my brothers forever; and to Lenira, my godmother, and Mazazi, my second godfather, who both represent me with Egúngún. Much gratitude to my spiritual family for their support, who made me feel at home from the very first visit; to Ìyá Ogum Bonam, one of my many "mothers"; and all my godbrothers and godsisters at Xango Cá Te Espero. Thank you to Veronica and my goddaughter Zenaide (*ibaye*—may she rest in peace) for being my mouth and ears in navigating Portuguese at the *terreiro*.

Special thanks to Jennifer Griffith, my first editor, who took me to task constantly and made this work much better than it would have been.

Thanks to the great screenwriter Ed Solomon, my good friend who helped me get over mental hurdles and shared his successful writing strategies, and Tim Page, who gave me another critical writing strategy. Thank you to my good friend Paul Austerlitz, one of my initial readers who offered many inspiring insights and constant encouragement.

To Ivor Miller, who provided constant encouragement and support, I owe a deep debt of gratitude for many things: providing access to the Smithsonian Library and accommodation (and becoming fast friends after two weeks); his generous editorial commentary as first reader; the numerous articles and obscure references concerning Egúngún that I would find in my inbox whether he was in Sweden or Cross River; and for his constant encouragement and uplifting support. His input and guidance improved this work immensely; it is a much better book having been steered by his keen perceptions.

Many thanks to Professor Luciana Barbosa de Souza and her father, author Ailton Barbosa de Souza, who helped me navigate my second visit to the *terreiro* and who have provided constant help in answering my many queries.

And thank you to Luiza Inah Vidal, who sent from Brazil the incredibly kind gift of the book *Obaràyí*, a resource which turned out to be fundamental to the last part of this book.

And finally, to Craig Gill, Lisa McMurtray, Valerie Jones, Todd Lape, and the full team at University Press of Mississippi for taking on this work and guiding it to fruition.

FOREWORD

—Robert Farris Thompson

Red cloth flies in the face of death. Ritually dressed phantoms from the past light up the world of the living. Technicolor heavenly visitors whirl magnificently as the *igbala* panels open up to deliver 1,000 points of information.

Egúngún. Citizens of heaven—*ará ọ̀run*—the returning ancestors, transporting love and blessings as they are called back to participate in earthly matters. What is Egúngún? The returned kings, the founders and leaders of the Yorùbá, they represent the collective ancestry, forming an unbroken path to ancient memory. Fantastically dressed in multiple layers of brilliant cloths, they deliver messages of moral righteousness, dispensing judgment, cleansing the community of evil, advising the people, making barren women fertile. It is tradition, a Yorùbá tradition.

In this wonderful book, Willson breaks down the history of Egúngún as it was carried to Brazil and tells the story of its powerful continuity on the island of Itaparica, and its eventual migration to Rio de Janeiro. He brings forth information we have not seen before. His story centers around *Xango Cá Te Espero*, the first Egúngún temple in Rio de Janeiro, and its historic origins in Itaparica, Bahia, brought to Rio from there by Aildés de la Rocha, a major African-Brazilian priestess and architect of Candomblé of the twentieth century.

I first met Brian Willson in 1985 when I was lecturing at Brooklyn College, where he was a graduate assistant. He was also a recently initiated priest of Ọbàtálá, and we hit it off immediately;

our friendship grew from that point. Later, in 2005, he told me he was headed to São Paulo to lecture, and I immediately informed him of *Xango Cá Te Espero*. Armed with this information, he indefatigably pursued its connection to Egúngún.

It is to here, at *Xango Cá Te Espero*, that Willson has spent over ten years going back and forth, learning Portuguese, establishing a familial relationship with the members of the *terreiro* (temple) and their spiritual leader—Aildés's son Babá Carlos Ojé Dúdú, and subsequently going through several initiations and *obrigaçãos*, eventually entering into the priesthood of Egúngún.

Xango! Cá Te Espero! *And this is where we wait for him.* A poetic moniker for the home of Xango, informed by readiness, devotion, faith, and action. It is not mere happenstance that the first temple of Egúngún is likewise dedicated to Xango; they enjoy a systemic relationship. With his pointed lappets of death-defying red, Xango, like Egúngún, is a protector, defender, and moral arbiter. It is here that Xango thrives next to Oya and Egúngún, Babá Égun with his separate secret grove and *igbàlę*, and Oya and Xango with their individual *barracão*, where the faithful participate in both secret initiations and public festivals.

I knew Carlos from the 1980s, when I discovered the *terreiro* and met his mother Aildés, the pioneering priestess responsible for this great emigration of Egúngún to Rio de Janeiro. In December 1986 in Rio I came across a small red book that documented the name and address of every Candomblé in Rio de Janeiro, Niteroi, and the northern suburbs. I was much intrigued by this text and swore to visit as many of the Candomblé that it listed as possible, but suddenly I noticed the name of a Candomblé in Jacarepaguá—Xango Cá Te Espero: *Thunder God, we are here awaiting your presence.* This intrigued me, because it announced not only the Candomblé but its principal action, the descent from the skies of the great thunder–lord, Xango Alado. Something was guiding me obviously, maybe Xango himself, something guiding me straight to Rio and then beyond to the suburb of Jacarepaguá.

And so began my rich and wonderful relationship with Aildés Batista Rocha and her son Carlos.

But I was not traveling alone. I was traveling with my son Clark and he had gone with me to the ancient Yorùbá settlement of Ketu, where he had seen Egúngún in action. He was thrilled and said, "Dad, listen, there is Egúngún here!" Clark was the one that recognized the *ìjímèrè* sound instantly—the sound of Egúngún that mimics the *ìjímèrè*—the patas monkey. You could not see the Egúngún immediately, but the sound instantly indicated their presence, that there were Egúngún in this house. And then suddenly one of them appeared, with the lappets gleaming with multiple images of owls, an allusion to the great mothers; the connection is with the night, the power of the night, medicines of the night, multiple knowledges of the night. I knew that one of the great adventures of my life was about to begin.

And I thought: *how can that be possible here in Rio de Janeiro? . . . They are supposed to only be on the island of Itaparica.* Which is what everyone was told and what they wanted to believe.

There began our friendship and from that moment on, every time I came to Brazil all during the 1990s I went straight to Casa Espero. There was an instance one time we were in a rental car and an Égun came out and blessed us, by activating his lappets and creating this wonderful divine wind that passed over the car and blessed me and my research assistant. This thrilled me—the idea of a Hertz rent-a-car being blessed by ancient Egúngún—cementing the idea of how structured the control of two worlds was.

Willson relates his own story of inspiration and persistence at uncovering the narrative of Egúngún in Brazil. He brings to light the history of Egúngún and genealogy from slave times to the present, as only one fully dedicated to Òrìṣà could do: investigating, observing, learning the language, and—most importantly— able to report as a participant with a deep spiritual understanding already in place, as a long-standing priest of both Ọbàtálá and

Ifá. Armed with this spiritual background, he understands and relates on multiple levels to the spiritual significance of Egúngún: he does not report solely from the academic observational mode. He is an *Amuxian*—a fully ranked Egúngún initiate, confirmed by members of the Egúngún society. Willson is clearly moved by his experiences and takes the reader along with him into his moments of elucidation and enlightenment.

There is something about Black culture: they know how to honor their dead. All the Black world—Yorùbá, Asante, Kongo— all these civilizations, they honor their dead with cloth. Cloth is the currency. You pile it up: clothes for the ancestor, over and over again you see cloth is the proper medium for letting the ancestors know that you love them, the most proper sacrifice to the dead. And Egúngún is completely out of that tradition. For the Yorùbá, what is Egúngún but the many honorific givings of ritual loyalty to the cause, and giving cloth to the ancestors.

As the Yorùbá established their classical religion across the waters in the New World despite the horrors of the Atlantic slave trade, in the ever-brilliant, resourceful, improvisatory mind of the Yorùbá, the tradition of ancestor veneration, coupled with a deep spiritual yearning, could not be vanquished. It materialized most efficaciously in the system of spiritualism of Allen Kardec—the "white table" misas, or séances, adopted as a means of maintaining contact with and veneration of the dead, thus filling the void.

We see aesthetic flashes of Egúngún throughout the diaspora. It's not quite true to say Egúngún didn't come to Cuba, because all the Egúngún colors—the reds, the yellows, the greens—all the colors are placed there in the shrines. In my book, *The Face of the Gods*, there is a glorious photograph by Chris Munnelly of an Oya altar with a feast for the dead showing a stream of colored cloths with the nine colors of Oya. It was like the Égun in miniature, the idea of Egúngún related to cloth and different colors and patterns, displayed on the wall above the offerings, tied to a faucet. One of the guiding footmarks are these altars to Égun. That's enough to bring back Égun. When we look at that altar we see it's like an Egúngún flattened out; the abstract essence of it is alive in Cuba.

But in Brazil Egúngún *did* flourish in all its powerful continuity, with all its beauty and complexity, retaining the necessary ritual information and ceremony. Willson brings forth a wealth of information. He illuminates the structural hierarchy of the Brazilian Egúngún, along with its rigorous discipline and secrecy, brought to life by stunning photographs of the *terreiros* and the Egúngún themselves.

As his godmother was destined to bring Egúngún from Africa, Willson is continuing this legacy of ashé—*the power to make things happen*—from Africa through Brazil, faithfully disseminating the knowledge of Egúngún.

—Robert Farris Thompson
New Haven
18 October 2020

A NOTE ON ORTHOGRAPHY

The diacritic marks of the Yorùbá language were not preserved in their written form in the diaspora; the original Yorùbá is written utilizing four different languages: Portuguese, Spanish, Lukumí (Yorùbá as spoken in Spanish Cuba), and English.[1]

Different tribes, commonly grouped together as Yorùbá, maintained their language, ritual prayers, incantations, and songs to the best of their ability under stark conditions, as a resistance to assimilation into the culture of the European enslavers.

The Yorùbá writing system based on the Roman alphabet, utilizing the diacritics (diacritical marks), started in the 1860s.[2] The Yorùbá alphabet contains four letters not found in English:

gb—articulated together
ẹ—as *e* in *get*
ọ—as *aw* in *jaw*
ṣ—as *sh* in *she*[3]

When captured phonetically, reproducing the ṣ sound (equivalent to *sh* in English—using *Ṣàngó* as an example), results in three iterations, plus the original. The ṣ is produced in Portuguese by the letter *X*, as in *Xango*. In English this transliterates to *Shango*, and in Spanish to *Chango*, as Spanish has no *sh* sound.

Furthermore, Yorùbá is a three-tone language; depending on the accent marks or lack thereof, words can have multiple meanings. The accent grave (à) indicates the low tone, the accent acute (á), the high tone; the middle tone has no accent.

For example: *bàtà* means *shoe*, while with different tonal markings, *bàtá* denotes the *drum* (belonging to the deity Ṣàngó). If *bata* is presented without tone marks the reader can only guess at its meaning by context.

The recalled spoken Yorùbá of the diaspora was transcribed with countless phonetic variations; thus the meanings of individual words were in many cases obscured. This led to incomplete or erroneous transcriptions of the prayers, songs, and ritual language, often resulting in multiple versions. As such, accurate translation of these phonetic speculations is difficult or impossible.

Following Miller, Manfredi, et al., I strongly advocate the use of the appropriate diacritics when known.[4] It is respectful of the language and culture—and also of the African reader—to reproduce the language faithfully and accurately.

For all Yorùbá words I use Abraham's standard orthography of the Ọ̀yọ́ dialect, and retain the tonal and diacritic markings.[5]

Certain words were problematic. Not wishing to impose Yorùbá spellings on Portuguese iterations of Yorùbá words, I retained the Portuguese where it is part of a quote or proper name, or as it appeared in a source, and in transcriptions of my interviews with Babá Carlos.[6] The word Babá (father) is one such example. In reviewing my Portuguese sources, Babá is consistently spelled with an acute accent on the last syllable, whereas in Yoruba it is written Bàbá. I have elected to use the Portuguese spelling throughout the text for consistency's sake.

In the instances where it is valuable to have both the Yorùbá and Portuguese version of a word, I indicate this as such:

Yorùbá [Y]
Portuguese [P]

Mo posese-posesee,
Owoóò mi ò Àkànbí.
Babaá wá diná run kò tiè kú mó.
Babaá wá sí tiè dòòrùn,
Eyí ta ó fi sáso gbe kalé.
Àkànbí ire lálèdé run.

I trotted and trotted,
I couldn't reach Àkànbí anymore.
Our father has transformed into a heavenly light that never dies.
Our father has even been transformed into a sun,
Whose rays shall dry our clothes.
Àkànbí, rest in peace.[7]

PART I

Never Too Late

Chapter 1

INTRODUCTION

From Long Island to Brazil

I was born on Long Island, New York, in the heart of the post–World War II baby-booming American dream. That I would eventually be drawn to and end up initiated in an African diaspora religious tradition at a significant level would have seemed completely far-fetched—and to some probably seems so to this day.

But I did end up here. I had no purposeful trajectory, but I did have an intuitive attraction to Black culture, mainly through the music. In the eighth grade I witnessed my first live concert: James Brown and the Fabulous Flames—two drummers, sparkled capes, a killing band, and all the regal showmanship inherent in that particular strain of the Black aesthetic. The airwaves were saturated with "In A Cold Sweat" and "I Feel Good"; but experiencing JB from thirty feet away—well, that was borderline religious. That concert surely fired some new synapses in my brain, expanding my sense of *possibilities*. I was already a drummer and music fanatic: between James, Hendrix, and the Chambers Brothers—announcing that "Time has Come Today" and hipping me to the distant land of Uptown Harlem—it was clear even at fourteen years old, my spirit felt a special link to the Black world.[1] Later Tony Williams, Jack DeJohnette, and Elvin Jones would solidify my musical/spiritual relationship with jazz, for me the pinnacle of Black culture.

The 1960s was the hippie era, but we were not particularly hip to a lot of important things, and the term *multicultural* had yet to be coined. As much as we loved Black culture, I did not know one Black person, simply because none lived in my town; they lived in the next town over, which the white population subconsciously (or otherwise) avoided. My family scraped by with the appearance of a middle-class existence, and the inherent racial views of that middle-class suburban mindset were powerful. Fortunately, my friends were both interesting and intelligent, and able to willfully transcend prejudicial viewpoints. This is all to say that, aside from music, I grew up with no special insight or avenue into Black culture.

I was never much of a student and studied little in high school; I gave little thought to college, though pressured to do so. After graduating high school, I worked in a record store and then a hip music club called My Father's Place, continuing to immerse my life in music. I made a pilgrimage to California, then spent a year in Chicago (where I had a brief stint as drummer with Bobby Cole and the Soul Shockers). It was here in Chicago that my horizons were forever widened with a paradigm-shifting concert by Sun Ra and an introduction to the music of Cecil Taylor,[2] as well as that of the AACM, the Association for the Advancement of Creative Musicians, a burgeoning collective for cutting-edge Black music. (Years later I would record with AACM member and master trumpeter Rasul Siddik.[3])

In 1977 I decided to go to college, and found a home at the State University of New York at Old Westbury, one of the only schools at the time offering a degree in jazz performance. This was an immersive experience into Black culture, at least as it existed in a college setting. My degree was in African American music performance; it was there that I would meet teachers and musicians who would inspire my life even to this day: Warren Smith, Andrei Strobert, Richard Harper, and Sinclair Acey. This was also where I would meet Betty Barney, my future godmother, when I registered for a class called African Dance and Drum. I did not know this was basically a class in Yorùbá culture, or that my teacher was a highly regarded priestess of the Òrìṣà Ṣàngó—the Yorùbá thunder god (Òrìṣà of thunder, owner of the drum). She would eventually initiate me into the mysteries of Òrìṣà and Santería (the Yorùbá religious tradition as practiced in Cuba) and give me my first hint into the meaning of Egúngún. Betty was already an advocate for African traditionalism and had started to take trips to West Africa to add traditional Nigerian Yorùbá religious training to her Cuban-based Santería foundation. This inclusive approach to studying the Yorùbá religion was reflected in her class.

I hounded Betty one day after class about some ongoing health problems I was having, based on previous private discussions of metaphysical healing. She asked, "Did I tell you I'd take a look at it?" I replied that she hadn't (nor did I know what she meant). From there we made an appointment for me to go to her house at 91 South Portland St. in Fort Greene, Brooklyn. (This was the Fort Greene of 1977, when hookers and hustlers walked the neighborhood streets, not hipsters heading for the gentrified cafes of millennial times.) "*Take a look at it*" meant reading me with the Yorùbá *dilogun* (cowrie shell) divination system; during the process she proceeded to uncannily spread my life out before me.[4] The reading seemed to last for several hours. Betty told me there was something I needed to do but was not ready to do: to complete the first-step initiation within Santería, the receiving of the beads called *ilèkès*. She was right; I wasn't ready. But as I left her home I felt a new, deep sense of belonging such as I had never felt before.

Even though I was not ready to receive my *ilèkès*, she took me on as an acolyte and introduced me to the world of *espiritismo*, the Cuban/Puerto Rican expression of spiritism. According to Brandon: "*espiritismo* is a variant of European spiritism" founded by Allan Kardec.[5] I began accompanying Betty to spiritist sessions in individuals' homes run by *espiritistas* (spiritist or medium) called *misas* or *centros* (a type of séance, for lack of a better term). This mediumistic communication with the spirit world was the way ancestor veneration was expressed in the diaspora—in lieu of the Egúngún society, which had not been established in Cuba or the United States. I first witnessed full-trance mediumship at these sessions; our participation took us to Brooklyn, New Jersey, and elsewhere. I had begun the long and arduous process of training as a spiritist medium.

It took me two years before I decided to finally get my *ilẹ̀kẹ̀s*. On my way to Betty's to tell her of my decision, I stopped and sat on a bench outside Fort Greene Park, moderating a final internal debate. I *was there*; the decision had been made. All of a sudden Betty and one of her godchildren walked by; happily surprised, she asked: "Brian, what are you doing here?" I replied by telling her of my decision. Soon after, I received my *ilẹ̀kẹ̀s*. With this ceremony I officially joined her *cabildo* (or "house," meaning the temple and its members)[6] and became an *ahijado*, or godson of the house.

Within three months of receiving my *ilẹ̀kẹ̀s* my chronic health issue disappeared. Within six months I had a new circle of friends. It is beyond the scope of this brief introduction to delve deeper into this initiation, but I mention these two outcomes to at least partially illuminate the weighty effects of this ceremony.

As members of Betty's house we were well trained in *espiritismo*; our house became known for our *espiritista* work. Some *cabildos* did not have the same level of expertise in this area; therefore we were often called upon to visit other houses to consult for their members. To be a spiritist medium is an incomparable experience, one that a few sentences or paragraphs cannot begin to cover.[7] She called us *egunistas*, fashioning her own hip moniker to include the Yorùbá word for spirit.[8] During one of our sessions, not long after I received my *ilẹ̀kẹ̀s*, I was to experience trance mediumship.[9] Thus began my lifelong relationship with the dead.

I had a great longing for this thing called Santería and Òrìṣà. I would take the two-hour train ride from Long Island to see my godmother, not even knowing if she would be home. Many times Betty's phone was disconnected—no money, no phone. I would take the chance and get on the train to Brooklyn. I was nothing if not hopeful and persistent; I'd knock on her door and if no one answered I'd sit on the stoop and wait around till she returned home. This is how serious I was to learn about Òrìṣà.

Òrìṣà and Egúngún resonated so genuinely with me; at the same time I was the ultimate outsider. Occasionally referred to as "the white boy" (not without love) or "my blue-eyed soul-brother," I was accepted to varying degrees by the practitioners of the religion. I was reluctant to share any part of my involvement with Santería with my family or anyone else; only a small circle of friends knew of my participation. My attitude changed over the years to some extent, but in many ways I lived a dual life. But my relationship with my *cabildo* was a big part of my life; Betty was a brilliant woman, kind, warmhearted, and welcoming. I felt I had a real home in this religion and in my house of godbrothers and godsisters. I could fill many chapters with stories of my lengthy relationship.

Fast-forward seven years and a lot of history. In July 1985 I *made ocha*—that is, I became an ọmọ Òrìṣà, a child of the Òrìṣà, an initiated priest of Ọbàtálá.[10]

When I became involved in Santería, it was a very secretive, closed society, empowering the Black and Latino community, not only spiritually but also on pragmatic levels. Black Americans now had a rare, powerful connection to African gods that was changing people's lives in remarkable ways. And it was something that was unconditionally theirs and theirs alone.

The Santeros and Santeras that initiated me were part of the earliest generation of the Black community initiated in the United States. They were the backbone of the Black Òrìṣà community. Betty told me she initially encountered resistance to initiating a white person. But she found her support with her confidante in the community, Alfred Davis—Omi Toki—and he agreed to run the ceremony. As the ceremony proceeded, I experienced acceptance simply as a child of Òrìṣà. Nevertheless, it was controversial. Not one to shy away from controversy, Betty was a pioneer and was following her destiny. According to her, in the weeks that followed, my ceremony was "the talk of the Òrìṣà circuit!"[11]

Eleven years later I was initiated as a *babaláwo*—or "father of secrets"—and I entered into lifelong commitment to studying Ifá divination and ritual.[12] Now, in 2020, I am an elder in my community, and I am a senior priest within the Yorùbá temple Ilé Okànràn Onílè, based in Ibadan and New York City, headed by the Awise of Idoland, Ibadan, Nigeria, Chief Adewale Bógunmbè.

I have never thought in terms of being a pioneer or breaking racial barriers. Òrìṣà was simply where I felt at home; I believed without any doubt that this was my destiny. The pull of the Òrìṣà was very potent and I followed my instincts. This resonated with a truism that Betty often reminded us of: "You don't choose Òrìṣà, the Òrìṣà choose you." Though I entered the religion as an outsider in 1977, in retrospect I look at that moment as that of a returning son.

If I was a pioneer at all, it is because I was part of a generation of Òrìṣà worshippers who were pioneers, Black Americans who grabbed hold of the Yorùbá religion with an indomitable strength. They created a base of knowledge, ritual, and tradition for this way of life to continue and flourish. My godmother Betty Barney, Ṣàngó Funké; my *adjubona* (secondary godmother) Cheryl Heyward, Omí Kio Ladé; my *oriate* (leader of ceremonies) Alfred Davis, Omí Toki; Jose Manuel, Ọya Dina (*oriate* for countless Òrìṣà initiations); and Arnaldo Carnero, one of my teachers, knowledgeable priest of Ṣàngó—these are just a few of the now-honored ancestors who stood at the forefront of the Òrìṣà tradition, and maintained the pillars of knowledge and gradation for future generations to come. *Ibae, bayén, bayén tonu*[13] to these honored ancestors.

It was a generation of firsts.

Decades later in Brazil, in 2006 I would meet Babá Carlos Ojé Dúdú, a brilliant Candomblé leader who subsequently would lead me into the mysteries of Egúngún, the Yorùbá secret society responsible for the veneration of the ancestors. Candomblé is the Yorùbá religion as practiced in Brazil—a diasporic sister to Santería/Lukumí.[14] Ojé Dúdú is the *alágbà* (elder leader) of the *terreiro* (Candomblé temple), Xango Cá Te Espero.[15] I met Babá Carlos through my friend and mentor, Robert Farris Thompson. In initial conversations with him, we discussed the state of Egúngún in the United States, my late godmother's legacy, and the possibility of my own initiation and training in Egúngún.

My initial visit to Brazil was as a guest lecturer speaking on music improvisation at UNICAMP, in São Paulo. I promised myself I would also visit Rio de Janeiro and Bahia while I was in Brazil, not knowing when I'd have this chance again. After my lecture obligations, I first traveled to Rio. The idea of a book had not germinated yet, though I was armed with a strong intellectual and spiritual curiosity to understand Candomblé and Egúngún. (I was *not* armed with a geographical knowledge of Rio, nor did I speak Portuguese.)

Thompson had informed me that I would find Egúngún in Jacarepaguá, a neighborhood in the outlying area of Rio. Only after several visits to Brazil did the idea of a book emerge. During one of my meetings with Thompson—after I had shown him the photographs from my most recent visit in 2008—he emphatically stated: "You've got to write a book." This inspired me and solidified the idea. I approached Babá Carlos about this. He loved the idea of a book and gave me full permission to write of my experiences and what I had learned there.[16] I had been keeping an informal journal from my first visit. I knew going forward it would be crucial for me to document everything more carefully. My spiritual quest and involvement now took on a whole other aspect. I recount my experiences at the terreiro in the first section of the book.

I was not armed with anthropological or ethnographic theory or jargon, or any particular methodology. However, I had completed a doctorate in music at the CUNY Graduate Center in NYC; I understood academic discipline. My methodology was one of practicality and common sense. One could say my approach was that of participant/observer, combined with a sense of naïveté. One thing I was sure of: to the best of my ability, I would not attempt to explain Brazilian Candomblé/Egúngún experiences based on my own outlook and spiritual training; I had to let these practices speak for themselves. At times when I thought an experience could neatly fit in my mental paradigm, it was set on its head on my next visit, or even the next day.

As a longtime student and adherent of African diaspora traditions, I had read most of the major works on the Yorùbá religion. I was very familiar with Thompson, Miller, Drewal, Bascomb, Brandon, Brown, and other writers of the African diasporic religious traditions. As I commenced my research and the process of writing I reviewed these works, and searched out literature on Egúngún to complement my experience and to consider my place among my predecessors.

There is a notable absence of material related to Egúngún in works about Òrìṣà and Santería. Although ancestor veneration is often referenced briefly, the Egúngún society gets little or no mention. Two works stand apart: *Oyá* by Judith Gleason and *African Art in Motion* by Robert Farris Thompson. Both reference Egúngún in Africa. Also, notably, George Brandon's *Santeria from Africa to the New World: The Dead Sell Memories* evidences a profound understanding of Egúngún through his stirring and important depictions of Black ancestry and the psychological and spiritual consequences of slavery vis-à-vis the ancestors. His perspective is moving and thought provoking. Other writers in the Òrìṣà tradition have addressed ancestor veneration as it was reimagined through spiritism in the diaspora.[17]

Although the existing Egúngún research is almost exclusively related to Africa, I found that research essential to help understand Egúngún's origins and relate to what I was experiencing in Brazil. These studies were oriented toward the Yorùbá-speaking region of Nigeria, and contain descriptive and historical observations, along with the cataloging and classification of the many different types of Egúngún from different areas. I found the most fruitful source in numerous articles, particularly the collection in Henry Drewal's classic 1978 *African Arts* issue dedicated to Egúngún.[18] This invaluable research, though almost exclusively etic in nature, holds great insight into the philosophy of the Yorùbá people and ancestral veneration through the Egúngún society. (To my knowledge, no emic study—inside the social group—exists from the point of view of a North American initiate.)

Additionally, I researched multiple works and articles concerning slave routes and points of origin, and intercontinental travel during and after the slave trade. This was critical to more deeply understand African heritage, continuity, and adaptation, as it related to the endurance of the Yorùbá people, the progenitors and guardians of Egúngún.

The majority of works regarding Egúngún in Brazil are in Portuguese; there is a notable absence of research in English. The essential article by Juana and Deoscoredes M. Dos Santos, *Ancestor Worship in Bahia*, is an invaluable exception.[19] By the same author mentioned above but in Portuguese, Juana Dos Santos's *Os Nágôs e Morte* (The Nágô and Death) is also an important source.[20] Though not readily available, the excellent *Obaràyí*, by Agnes Mariano, is a significant work concerning the life of Balbino Daniel de Paula, a *pae-de-santo* (father of the saint—a Candomblé Òrìṣà priest) of a major terreiro—the subject is a descendant of an important Egúngún family in Itaparica.[21] *Obaràyí* contains stunning photography; it is in Portuguese, but

Mariano supplies a wonderfully complete English translation as an appendix.

Two lengthy interviews with Babá Carlos were invaluable for both the esoteric information and his personal family history; the initial interview is reproduced in the final chapter.[22] Numerous interviews with Thompson afforded me a rare personal insight to Egúngún in Africa and Brazil, and inspired many deep discussions of African continuity in Brazil, Cuba, and the United States.

The recorded interviews with Babá Carlos were held in Portuguese with real-time translation. My translator and friend, Viviane da Porto, though fluent in Portuguese, was not completely familiar with Candomblé terminology, so it was understandably necessary to pause and clarify at times. This occasionally would break the flow of the interview. Topics went by quickly; some things I did not understand fully in the moment. For the second interview, my initiation brother Fabio did his best translating, somewhat aided by my still-rudimentary Portuguese. When I would ask Carlos to re-explain something, it was frustrating for both of us: "Hey! Let's keep going; I'm a young mind in an old body!" I was breaking his train of thought. I had both interviews re-translated and transcribed when I returned to the United States; they benefited greatly from the second translation.

I narrate my experiences based on my journals, as other authors of the African diasporic tradition have done.[23] This was a very natural approach for me. The idea for a book came gradually to me; as noted, I did not initially pursue Egúngún as a writing topic.[24] My foremost objective was my personal spiritual growth through Egúngún initiations; my writing interweaved simultaneously with my activities. It later became clear that writing was becoming a fundamental part of my being there, but I never felt like an outside observer; I never experienced that duality.

When I first arrived in Brazil, I had been initiated in Ifá/Òrìṣà for many years; my initiatory status found acceptance, with some parallel equivalents, and was acknowledged and respected. This acceptance allowed me insider status to any of the ongoing Òrìṣà activities; only in Egúngún did I have ritual boundaries I had to observe according to my level of initiation (or lack thereof). My personal comfort level increased as I traveled there more often to continue my Egúngún ceremonies and initiations. I grew closer to my spiritual family. I was also slowly learning Portuguese, which was of obvious, vital benefit. I was well on my way to Egúngún initiation by the time I began formally writing this work. This all allowed me to report from an emic viewpoint. I was a priest and a seeker first, then a writer. In the area of Egúngún, of course, I was a novice.

During my time in the terreiro, I attempted to write as complete a diary as possible, initially for my own recollection and later more assiduously for the book. In the process of transcribing and reviewing my journals, a memory would blossom and expand, providing new information and perceptions to augment my notes. These might reveal additional recollections, as well as new perceptions of my mental and emotional state as I traveled back in time to that moment.

Drawing on my personal emotions and experiences, I seek to take the reader beyond the veil of mere description and illuminate the numinous or unseen qualities of an event or state of being. My goal is not mere reportage, but rather to bring forth the hidden metempirical aspects, to share on the deepest personal level, and most of all to illuminate Egúngún, its adherents, its beauty, its importance.

What does it mean for a white male North American to write authentically about an African diasporic tradition? Though I hold the cultural influences of Western and American peoples, I've traversed a long path from the "ultimate outsider" to become a member of an African Brazilian diasporic tradition. I felt that race held little significance among my terreiro brothers and sisters. After each visit to Brazil I would become a little more comfortable socially—especially as my Portuguese improved. Outside of the terreiro, the *cariocas* and Bahians that became my friends revealed an openhearted easiness to living that was a constant revelation to me. Their sense of how to live affected me in the best possible way.

The background story of my book is thus: I am a middle-class North American who became initiated by a Black American who brought Egúngún from Nigeria to Brooklyn. I'm reporting on a culture that I plausibly consider, as James Murphy eloquently states, "more authentic and noble than my own."[25] My task involves transmitting the mystical depth and powerful meaning Egúngún has for its devotees, so that the reader might catch a glimpse of the spiritual fulfillment that an adherent would feel. I believe this is the most important aspect of my work. If my background story is valuable to this study it is because, as Ivor Miller states: "The vision of grassroots effort to transcend race and class through a common spiritual practice is an important story for our society today, where division and suspicion are the national themes."[26]

This book is the culmination of a ten-year relationship with Babá Carlos, my initiations and personal involvement there, my interviews, research, and numerous trips to Brazil, where I have become a member of the terreiro extended family. These initiations and relationships allow me to relate the story of Egúngún from an insider's point of view; in addition to my research and reportage, my work is informed by what Thompson calls "respect for your lived expertise."[27]

A FORCED MIGRATION

The brutality of slavery tore apart the culture, way of life, familial structure, and religious traditions of Africans through the forced migration of the Middle Passage to the Americas.[28] But where the volume and duration of the slave trade were large and protracted, much was also retained—in particular in Brazil, Cuba, and Haiti, where expressions of African belief systems were maintained, known as Candomblé, Santería (Lukumí) and Vodun, respectively.

Brazil received over four million unwilling participants in this migration—about 44 percent of the total forced relocation from Africa—throughout the four centuries of the slave trade (1501–1866).[29] During the period from 1810–1851—the era when the earliest Candomblé and Egúngún houses were founded—more than half the slaves taken from the Slave Coast to the Americas landed in Bahia.[30] This provided a concentration of slaves from West Africa who brought with them their religious beliefs and rituals. According to Eltis, Yorùbá traditions dominated nineteenth-century slave communities in Bahia.[31] It was here in Bahia on Itaparica Island—situated directly across the Bay of All Saints (Baía de Todos os Santos)—that the Egúngún society would be reconstituted, reborn, and carefully maintained.[32]

Although the formalized structure of Egúngún was uniquely preserved only in Brazil, the spirit of the cult—that of ancestor veneration—was not lost in the diaspora, ingrained as it is in African tradition and culture. Ancestor veneration inevitably manifested in its own right. Thompson thus cautioned, "We must be careful not to say that Egúngún did not survive,"[33] because ancestor veneration and communication with the dead remained an essential part of all African diasporic spiritual traditions. It was reimagined and manifested in myriad forms: Kardecian spiritism; the white-table *misa* (or *centro*, séance) of Cuban and Puerto Rican influence; dedicated sacred ancestral spaces in the corners or bathrooms with the *òpá ikú* or Égun stick used to call upon the dead; and the use of ritual prayers to the ancestors said at the opening of all Lukumí ceremonies.[34] As a Cuban teacher of Ivor Miller's states, "In Cuba, without Égun, there is nothing."[35]

Furthermore, we see graveyard markers and other acknowledgments in the southern part of the United States, reflecting the honored status of the dead.[36] The rites of the Cuban *Abakua* society include full-body masks to represent ancestors,[37] while the Indian Mardi Gras outfits of New Orleans—with their elaborate costumes—echo the aesthetic of the magnificent *aṣọ* (*axo* [P], the dress of the Egúngún) of Brazil and Yorùbáland.[38] All of these exist to make possible veneration of and communication with those who have gone before us.

My story follows the vision and inspiration of my godmother, Betty Barney—the first person to bring Egúngún from Nigeria to the United States.[39] I trace the history of Egúngún as it exists in Brazil, and discuss the idea of continuity and change as the Egúngún society evolved on the island of Itaparica in Bahia, eventually migrating to Rio de Janeiro. This migration was accomplished through the efforts of Aildés Batista Lopes, mother to Babá Carlos, Ojé Dúdú, my godfather.

There is a common denominator between Egúngún in Yorùbáland and Egúngún in Brazil. Although there are multifarious manifestations of the Egúngún in Yorùbáland in terms of costume, function, and history—more varied than the insular tradition of the cult in Brazil—Egúngún share the definition as *ará ọrun*, translated as, "the people from beyond" or "members of heaven." The Egúngún societies on both continents share a common purpose: to maintain a highly disciplined and structured secret society that possesses the ability to summon ancestral forces that in turn bless the people, towns, and environs with good health, fecundity and prosperity; to provide for the continued relationship with those who have passed on, both as individual ancestors and as collective moral forces representing lineages of ancient leaders and protectors; to be moral arbiters for the community; and finally, to maintain a link into the spiritual world through annual communal rituals, cementing and maintaining the bond between the living and the dead.

Some witnesses and adherents of the Òrìṣà tradition here in the United States have witnessed the Brazilian Egúngún and were overwhelmed by both the visual spectacle and the spiritual power radiating from these multicolored ancestral messengers. In all my years of training and experience within the Ifá/Òrìṣà tradition, I too have experienced nothing like it. A knowledgeable American Òrìṣà priest and well-known author described the experience as humbling and awe-inspiring: ". . . as if I was walking down the street surrounded by the skyscrapers of Wall Street."[40] To be in the presence of Egúngún is a powerful and transporting experience, the striking visual impact of the mythically embroidered garments arrests one's mind, while the *abala* lappets fan forth in a cosmic whirlwind—this all offers a profound experience to the psyche, one to be reckoned with.

It was a great privilege to be initiated into the Egúngún society, and to be adopted by *minha família* in Brazil. I was given the title Oluwo Pássoro, at the culmination of my first ceremonial visit to the terreiro in September 2008, from the king of the Egúngún spirits at Xango Cá Te Espero: Babá Ọ̀lọ́jadé, whom I discuss in subsequent chapters.[41]

Two people were crucial to my interest and involvement in Egúngún: first my godmother, Betty Barney, priestess of Ṣàngó,[42] who set me on the path toward Egúngún through divination and my subsequent initiations. The second was Robert Farris Thompson, who encouraged me throughout. When I met Thompson in 1986, I had been initiated as a priest of Ọbàtálá for two years. We began communicating about all things concerning Òrìṣà and the Yorùbá religion; the first questions I asked were about Egúngún in Brazil. He informed me of the four existing temples, all located on the island of Itaparica. Thompson's communication, constant inspiration, and support eventually led me to Xango Cá Te Espero, where I encountered Egúngún firsthand in my search for connection to the inhabitants of heaven, *ará ọrun*.

Betty Barney planted the seed and informed me of my spiritual predisposition to the Egúngún cult. She continued her guidance through revelatory dreams and inspiration from *ọrun*, while

Thompson facilitated the initial connection through his inspired research in Brazil and Africa.

I have taken great care to ensure that I do not betray my initiatory oath of secrecy. To honor this, I have necessarily withheld some details of the Egúngún rituals, but I have shared as much of my personal state of mind as I felt comfortable. In addition to the historical knowledge and ceremonial descriptions, my underlying wish is to impart the profound sense of love, spiritual elevation, and familial camaraderie embodied in the veneration of the Egúngún by its adherents—novice, priest, and layperson alike. Part personal journal, part metaphysical mystery, part scholarly work, part reportage, this work relies on all of these approaches. If there are any mistakes, omissions, or erroneous information, the responsibility is mine alone.

I submit this work in service to the Egúngún society as it exists and is rigorously maintained in Brazil, and to all manifestations of Egúngún practice throughout the world. I hope that it helps fulfill my godmother's dream of uplifting our community by spreading the knowledge of Egúngún to the diaspora.

Chapter 2

DIARY 1 2006–2007

"She Is Standing Right Behind You"

JUNE 2006

My initial contact with Babá Carlos Ojé Dúdú was by cell phone. In the summer of 2006 I had been invited to give a master class on improvisation in percussion at UNICAMP (University of Campinas), in São Paulo. I had promised myself I would also visit Rio and Bahia; having been a student and adherent of the African diaspora religion of the Yorùbá for more than thirty years, I wished to learn more about Candomblé, the Brazilian rendering of that religion, brought to Brazil by enslaved Africans.

Before I left, I called Robert Farris Thompson. I knew he would guide me to the must-visit spots and, hopefully, provide some introductions. In his inimitable style he quickly rattled off the name Xango Cá Te Espero, the terreiro where they practiced Candomblé and Egúngún.[1] The only address I had was Rua Ourém in Jacarepaguá, and the name of the person to seek out: Babá Carlos, an *Ojé* [P] (high priest, *Òjè* [Y]) of the Egúngún society. I scribbled like mad, writing my phonetic version of what Bob fired off—not wanting to take up too much of his time—filling my yellow pad. I had no idea at the time what *Rua Ourém* meant (Ourém Street, in Portuguese) or where I would be going, but knew he had given me gold.

This was a rare referral from the horse's mouth: Thompson's studies of ritual arts and performance between West Africa and the Americas transformed the art historical scholarship in the late twentieth century and inspired generations of scholars, as well as artists and musicians, to explore African heritage as a positive contribution to the humanities.

Thompson also gave me information about Bahia and suggested I visit the terreiro of the famed *pae-de-santo* (priest, literally: father of the saint) Balbino Daniel de Paula, at Ilê Axé Opô Aganju,[2] in the municipality of Lauro de Freitas. I didn't fret much about showing up at places unable to speak the language. Because I had traveled extensively as a musician, I was used to being in unfamiliar places, often unable to speak the language of my host country, so the potential linguistic and communicative challenges were not too intimidating. And I have a pretty adventurous spirit.

Faced with the daunting task of finding Rua Ourem, I contacted my Brazilian goddaughter, Zenaide, who was living at the time in Itaguai, a town outside of Rio. Zen—a Fulbright scholar, completely fluent in both English and Portuguese—was an excellent tour guide and translator.[3]

I stayed in a worn-down hotel in Copacabana where Zenaide met me and we took a taxi heading south. We knew only that Jacarepaguá was a huge, sprawling suburb south of the city proper of Rio de Janeiro. After a spectacular ride down the coast, passing through many different neighborhoods and finally through Barra da Tijuca, we found our way into Jacarepaguá. Finding Rua Ourém was another story—we circled endlessly (no GPS or Google Maps) and asked directions at least ten different times until, just off the main road, we finally spotted a *very* faded painted sign on a wall that read: *Rua Ourém.*

Arriving at the terreiro, we knocked on the large, white iron gates of the entrance; on either side extended the tall white concrete walls that enclosed the terreiro, continuing to the left

Figure 2.1. Ọya's house. As you enter the terreiro you see Ọya's house; the path to the left leads to Xango's house, adjacent on the right.

Figure 2.2. Side view of Ọya's house. This building (along with Xango's house) is known as a *barracão*, where all formal ceremonial activities take place. These two large halls form the main structures of the terreiro, with smaller, ancillary buildings surrounding them. Babá Carlos's personal residence stands opposite Ọya's house.

straight down almost a full block, and to the right, curving around toward the back. A woman answered, who kindly informed us: "Babá is not here but we can try him on this phone." As we entered to converse briefly, we saw a house on the right and then a large red and white building on the left.[4] Later I would know this as Oya's house.

This was all we observed in our short time there. As the woman needed a ride to her job at the local mall, we offered her transportation in our taxi as we headed back to Rio; this gave us the opportunity at least to say hello to Babá Carlos on her phone. He graciously invited us back, saying he looked forward to the time when we might meet in person. We spoke of Thompson and his history with the terreiro. Thompson also knew Carlos's mother Aildés very well; she had founded the terreiro. This was my first introduction to Babá Carlos and the terreiro of Xango Cá Te Espero. At least we had each other's phone numbers now.

I had planted the seed to experiencing something spectacular, and I knew that next time I would find a way to continue this relationship. I was able to continue on to Bahia and there found a waiting audience for my master classes at Universidade Federale da Bahia (UFBA) and Pracatum—and a gracious host in the person of Prof. Jorge Baguina. He kindly took me to a Candomblé celebration at another terreiro, and I was also invited to and attended an *obrigação* (ritual obligation)[5] at Pai Balbino's terreiro, Ilê Axé Opô Aganju, the one Thompson had suggested I visit.[6] This was a remarkably cordial and enlightening visit, but I was eager to return to Brazil and visit again Xango Cá Te Espero in Jacarepaguá, and continue my search for Egúngún.

JUNE 2007: "SHE IS STANDING RIGHT BEHIND YOU"

I returned to Brazil the following year in June 2007, at the invitation of the Federal Universities in both Rio and Bahia, where I participated in several lectures and classes, and met with friends from previous trips. But the main venture and thrust of the trip was to continue my pursuit of knowledge at the terreiro. Arriving on Saturday June 23, I immediately got in touch with Xango Cá Te Espero. As it happened they were celebrating the annual festival for Xango that very night. Exhausted from travel, I opted to go visit the next day, the final day of the festival.

So, on Sunday, Zenaide and I returned to the terreiro for the last day of the annual Xango celebration. It was a beautiful winter day; we were greeted warmly and invited to stay for conversation, and to share a meal. We sat on some folding chairs outside the *barracão*—Oya's house, one of the ceremonial buildings of the temple. Sitting with my back to the wall of Oya's house and facing Babá Carlos, we engaged at length about Egúngún, with Zen effortlessly translating. Fluent in Portuguese and Yorùbá, Carlos did not speak any English; and I did not speak Portuguese or Yorùbá.

At one point one of the members of the terreiro came by and gave us a small piece of rubbery, tough flesh about the size of a fingernail to eat. Understanding that this was some part of ritual offering, I of course accepted. After about thirty seconds it felt as if I had ingested a drug, my whole world spun around for a moment. I must have looked alarmed, for Carlos asked me "Está bom?" (You okay?), and then explained that we had just eaten a piece of the lung of the turtle, which was fed to Xango, a standard practice, given to gain good health and strength in our own lungs. I said, "Oh okay, that makes sense!"[7]

The conversation turned to the Egúngún, a topic I have been fascinated by since my introduction to the religion. I had little knowledge of this subject, except through my godmother, whose story follows below.[8] Up until this point, I had been reluctant to discuss my personal history on the subject. But in this instance, I felt this was important to discuss with Babá Carlos, hoping that he would shed some light on the topic and share his opinion of my account of how Egúngún had manifested in America for the first time. So I told him my story.

ESTABLISHING EGÚNGÚN IN NORTH AMERICA: THE PIONEERING EVENT

My godmother in New York—Betty Barney, whose initiation name was Ṣàngó Fúnkẹ́[9] (*ibaye*)—was a great priestess of the Òrìṣà Ṣàngó (Xango [P] in Brazil). She was a true pioneer in the Yorùbá religion, particularly in the Black community of Brooklyn, and perhaps her greatest achievement was that she brought Egúngún to North America.[10] This had been her mission in life and she carried it out—though its success was limited. This "seating" or "planting" of Egúngún occurred in late fall, 1987. It was a controversial undertaking and not easily carried out, for reasons both logistical and financial. She did not have a lot of initial support from her initiation community, but eventually did. It was questioned—by some—as to whether or not she had the authority or sanction to initiate this pioneering ceremony.[11] No matter what, she completed her task. This was something that had been seen years before as her destiny by her godfather in Nigeria, the late *àràbà* (highest ranking *babaláwo*) of Lagos, Ifágbèmí Àjànàkú, who told her: "you will accomplish something great across the water."[12] In conversation she confided to me: "They told me in my *itá* (the life reading you receive when initiated) that I would do something very big; I thought maybe I would write a book. I never imagined it would be this."[13]

Several logistical aspects were involved in Betty's endeavor, not least of which was to build the *igbodu*,[14] the abode (basically a single concrete room) in which the Egúngún would be seated (or would live, as it were). This was the first step in bringing Egúngún to America; the physical representation (in Brazil *assento* [P], "seat") of the spirit of Egúngún needed accommodation outside the normal living area. (Egúngún cannot live inside with humans; this is the abode of the dead—therefore viewed as too dangerous to reside in a person's home.) Funds to build this dwelling house had not yet been raised and the time for the ceremony was soon approaching. I called Betty to tell her I would cover the expenses of building the concrete house for Egúngún. I was glad to do so. Although highly enthusiastic and wanting to be involved in the Egúngún ceremony—I had been a devotee of the religion[15] for many years—my participation otherwise was not possible, due to my travel schedule as a touring musician. So, this would be my contribution. She was thrilled and highly appreciative, having had no inkling how the necessary funds were going to be obtained.

When Betty visited me in Paris in late December 1987 (performing together there at the Magnetic Terrace—she was a wonderful singer), I learned I could not be a member or hold any chieftaincy title because of my absence at the ceremony. This would have been a great honor in my eyes, and thus was disappointing to me because of my great interest in Egúngún. I was touring at the time, so I did not dwell on it. Once the Egúngún was seated, societies known as *egbes* were formed, one male, one female. Both represented Egúngún, but I have no firsthand knowledge of what that membership entailed or its meaning.

Betty passed away on April 20, 1988, not long after the seating of Egúngún. In December 1991, my *adjubona, Omi Kio Lade* (Cheryl Heyward), passed away.[16] These events felt ominous to me. There was always an aura of uncertainty and a displaced, unfamiliar energy around this Egúngún, and, as our house dissolved with the passing of our leaders, I came to never speak about the Egúngún that was brought to Brooklyn. The few times I did, it seemed to produce a palpable sense of negativity.

However, now, sitting in front of an Egúngún specialist in Brazil, thousands of miles away from home, I was inspired to go ahead and tell this story to Babá Carlos Ojé Dúdú, so that he might understand what had occurred in America. I suppose I hoped for some illumination on the subject, too, but either way I was surprised to notice that for the first time I was comfortable in telling this story.

Betty had informed me early on of my close affinity with Egúngún. During my second reading[17] with *dilogun*, the sixteen cowrie shells used for Òrìṣà divination, she looked up from her mat and said, "Boy, you are a true child of Égun." The letter (an oracle signal achieved by the position of cowrie shells) thrown was Ọsá méjì.[18] As a beginner in this religion, I had no idea of what she was referring to. I would eventually learn about the world of the dead as I became more involved, and my curiosity about the Egúngún society never faltered. She firmly believed, she said, that if I went to Nigeria and Egúngún cult members met me, "they would want you to be in it."

I explained to Babá Carlos what little I knew about the seating of Egúngún that had taken place. My limited knowledge had come only after returning from a six-month tour, by which time almost all the necessary rituals had been completed, though I was able to participate in one offering to that Égun.[19] I also witnessed the first dancing of Egúngún in North America. This ceremony, held in a hall in Brooklyn in 1988, was witnessed by the various houses of the New York Òrìṣà community, the chiefs of the newly formed Egúngún Egbe, including Alfred Davis and Montego Joe, the newly formed Women's Egbe, and by Ọba Oseijeman Adéfúnmi and members of his temple from the Ọyọtúnjí Village in South Carolina.

As a well-regarded figure in the Black American Òrìṣà tradition, Betty had traveled numerous times to Nigeria to study with the late àràbà, Chief Ifágbèmí Àjànàkú.[20] Though deeply respectful of the knowledge she learned from the Cubans (Santería came from Cuba in the late 1950s),[21] she sought out the roots of her culture and fought vigorously for the Òrìṣà tradition's autonomy as an African religion, rather than as an adopted Cuban transplant.²² Her bringing of Egúngún from Nigeria—a purely African aspect of the Òrìṣà tradition—reinforced and reflected her outlook and goals. She was, however, faithfully respectful of and grateful for Cuban Lukumí (Santería) as it was embraced by the Black community; she told stories with the highest praise of those brave women and men who carried the religion from Cuba to the United States. In conversation one time she saluted these courageous Cuban women who made the perilous sea crossing "with their *dilogun* in their panties."²³

Betty saw the Egúngún society as a powerful tool to help all humankind, but her immediate concern was for the poor and disenfranchised of the Black American community. She was specifically concerned with the healing of the deep psycholog-ical trauma held over in the spiritual subconscious of all Black Americans: that of the slave experience and all that had followed in its wake. In conversation with me, and as memorialized in the commemorative program at her funeral, she stated: *The purpose of planting Egúngún here is to forever break the psychological chains of slavery for Black Americans.*

Betty had experienced the struggles of Black America firsthand, and for years was a mentor to young Black students through her activity as an acclaimed performer of African folkloric dance, and as a professor of African dance at the State University of New York at Old Westbury. She saw the religion of the Òrìṣà not only as a spiritual tool, but also as a means of empowerment. Her research and inspiration brought her to the Egúngún society, where she developed and intuited this idea of breaking through psychological boundaries and restraints by establishing the pow-erful spiritual tradition of Egúngún. She was convinced that the Egúngún tradition could repair the broken connection between African Americans and their ancestral roots in Africa, retrieving the link to the lost memory of the ancestral family, which had been severed by the abomination of slavery.

Figure 2.3. Memorial program from Betty Barney's funeral.

beckoned and in Nigeria, West Africa, in
December, 1971, Betty was initiated into the
Babalu-Aiye society of Orishas, at the
Compound of Ile Araba Fagbemi Ajanaku-Ibaye,
of Lagos.

She was proud of her memberships including
IFA Esin Adimula-Afrikan Religious
Archdiocese of West Africa. Title Reverend,
also chairperson of the N.Y. Order; Local
802, Musicians Union; Local 2190, United
Professors -- A.F.T.; ARSADA (member in good
standing) Nigeria; ARSADA MEJI-NY Chapter,
Vice President; Society of Orisa (from
1960); Egbe -- Seniority, Lago, Nigeria;
Society of Bata Drums (junior member).

While developing spiritually, Betty still
found time to play golf, make films (Ganja
and Hess; Tropicana and a Channel 13 educational piece), radio spots (WLIB, WBLS,
WBAI, WBGO, WPKN, and WIKM in Connecticut);
6 television appearances (Triboro Chevrolet
commercial, Moet Champagne commercial, Joe
Franklin Show . . .)

Betty, "Brooklyn's First Lady of Song" will
ever be with us. ✳Her happiest days were her
last ones, because she was able to see her
age long dream fulfilled; that is the
planting of the Egungun in North America.
Through her guidance, Baba Adeshina Awopimpe
Adimula of Lagos, Nigeria arrived in New
York and planted the Egungun, the Orisha of
the ancestors of decendents of Africa. The
Egungun had to be planted in North America,
Betty (Sango Funke) said, to break, forever,
the psychological chains of slavery
restraining the growth of African
descendants in America. Since the planting
of Egungun, the Chiefs of Egun have been
initiated and the Egbe Women's Society
established.

As I finished my story I reflected on an occurrence of the pre-vious night. I had had a lengthy dream concerning Betty and her youngest son Ifaladé.[24] I had recalled it with great clarity upon waking in my hotel room in Flamengo, a downtown section of Rio de Janeiro. The lucidity of the dream was not unusual—I had long become accustomed to dreams of great clarity—but the content was more than a little curious. In the dream, Betty (Ṣàngó Funké) appeared dressed in the magnificent red outfit of Ṣàngó, embroidered with gold lamé trimming—a majestic sight. A small crowd stood around her, across from where Ìyá (literally: mother, a customary priestess appellation) had appeared; Ladé was there, upset and crying. People were asking what the matter was, and I was telling them: "It's okay. He is just overwhelmed and happy because he sees his mother." I awoke from the dream wondering: "Okay, why in the world did I just dream about my godmother and her son, and a large public crowd, while I'm five thousand miles away from home?" I was soon to find out. I told Babá Carlos none of the dream right then, I just finished my story.

At this point, Carlos asked me: "Your godmother, was she a stout dark-skinned woman with large breasts?"

"Yes," I said.

"Oh, because I have just seen her standing behind you twice now."

He continued, observing, "Okay, she started the work with Egúngún but she wants you to finish it; that is what you are doing here. You must finish what she attempted to do, she was not able to see it through to its full fruition; it did not last. Her spirit followed you down here to make this connection."

As much as I loved Òrìṣà and Egúngún and Ifá, I was not prepared for Carlos's words. I was visiting the terreiro out of an ongoing interest in Yorùbá heritage, Egúngún specifically—which had been a closed mystery to me for so many years, and proba-bly would have remained so, outside of a trip to Yorùbáland. I had not expected such personal revelations, responsibilities, or

Figure 2.4. Photograph of Aildés Batista Lopes (Babá Carlos's mother) on the wall in Xango's barracão.

obligations. I was taken aback by Babá Carlos's profound state-ment and at the same time felt honored. *Now* I understood the dream of the previous night. Witnessing this turn of events—an introduction to Egúngún, a connection I had been looking for my whole life—manifest itself unexpectedly like this, far from home, surprised me greatly. I had resigned myself to probably

never achieving the dream of involvement with Egúngún, and
it was now a distinct possibility—though I had no idea how it
would all happen. Babá Carlos and I were just at the beginning
of our discussions. We were just talking; I had not yet witnessed
anything and I had no idea how Babá and his terreiro worked
with Egúngún. And I definitely didn't speak Portuguese.

Carlos then related the history of Xango Cá Te Espero and
talked at length about his mother, Aildés, who taught Yorùbá
and who had tutored him in the language since he was twelve
years old. (Carlos is completely fluent in Yorùbá and, of course,
Portuguese, his native language.) He had helped compile her
notes and lectures on Yorùbá.

After outlining the history of the terreiro, speaking highly of
Thompson and his friendship with Aildés, Carlos informed me
that he and the members of the terreiro would call Betty's spirit,
and that I would need to come back next weekend. I at first failed
to really grasp what he was saying, but it then dawned on me
that he literally meant to call her and manifest her spirit. I briefly
succumbed to a bewildered Americano mindset, explaining flight
problems and so forth, then quickly switched gears, saying not
to worry, and that I would work it out.

Babá Carlos explained that I would need Betty's birth and
death date. I thought this would be easy to accomplish, but it
turned out to involve numerous calls back home, setting my
patient wife to the task of calling all parties who might have
information, and finally obtaining the correct dates. Nothing was
easy! (One might think this was an obvious and available piece
of information, but it turned out not to be so.) I had to connect
with Betty's youngest son Ladé (and relay my dream to him),
who was kind and helpful, but he in turn had to do research. I
also had to open old connections with one of my godsisters—as
we had been estranged for many years. This turned out not to
be difficult, but it certainly caused old relationships, and some
old controversies, to resurface in one's memory. This in itself
was revealing, but not problematic or negative.

Figure 2.5. Two mountain landmarks en route to the terreiro.

Figure 2.6. Babá Carlos in Ọya's barracão standing next to the royal thrones of Egúngún.

I scrambled, changing flights and hotels, and completing other necessary tasks so as to accomplish this invocation of Betty's spirit—to witness her presence made possible by the sheer generosity of this near stranger. I felt honored to do so, but also that I had just entered into a huge obligation; I had stepped off the cliff and blindly proceeded, informed only by faith, inspiration, and nerve. I did not hesitate, however, a trait that has led me into trouble at times. But I could never ignore such clear messages from the spiritual world. With all the particulars now resolved, I waited patiently for the following Sunday to come, to honor, invoke, witness, elevate—and whatever else might happen—the spirit of my godmother, Ṣàngó Funké.

I must emphasize Babá Carlos's generosity, and the warmth and connection that existed between us from the moment we met, which continues to this day. With no warning, Babá had unhesitatingly gone out of his way to call all the members of his terreiro together to honor and communicate with Ṣàngó Funké. Though I had taken on an obligation based on faith alone, Carlos—who barely knew me—had immediately responded to the situation before him, and rearranged his schedule and that of others, in order to communicate with the spirit who had presented herself to him. He shouldered and fulfilled my request as an obligation of no small import: his was a much bigger task than the one I had committed to.

Chapter 3

DIARY 2 2007

"I Miss You Already" (*Eu já estou com saudades*)

Zenaide had arranged for a taxi to meet the two of us at the Central metro stop; from there we drove to the terreiro and arrived early afternoon. I had put aside money for the ritual—in hindsight a pittance—it was either $175 or 175 Brazilian *reals*. In both North America and Latin America, money that one typically gives as payment or offering for spiritual work is called by the Spanish term *derecho* ("ritual fee"); this amount would have been considered a very small derecho.

I had no idea what to expect. It was a bit of a roller-coaster ride I had committed to, informed by faith and my new feelings for this impressive person, Babá Carlos, and by love for my godmother, so I proceeded. I knew nothing of Egúngún; I had no concept of what we might be doing that day—other than from Babá's statement, "We will be calling her spirit," leaving me with a deep feeling of mystery, great anticipation, and wonder.

When we arrived in the afternoon, I gave Zen the derecho and she delivered it to Carlos. Previously Babá had told me that, in addition to ascertaining the birth and death dates, we needed to call Betty during the twilight hour—between afternoon and evening, as the day changed to night. At this in-between time, he noted, the door to the spiritual world is open: as we are between day and night, so would we also be between the worlds of the living and the dead. With little preamble, I was instructed to go

35

into a small kitchen area, and remove my socks and shoes. Once in the kitchen, I was led to a counter and told to dip my hands in a bowl of what I guessed was a mixture of white cornmeal and water. I was further instructed to pray to Şàngó Funké about my intention there. I prayed for her spirit and blessings, thanked her for all she had done for me in life, and prayed for the well-being of both her sons.

As soon as I had put my fingers in the mixture, I immediately entered a subtle trance state. I am not a stranger to trance or possession, or altered states of consciousness—having been trained as a spiritual medium.[1] But this occasion was very different; I was *muito tranquilo*, calm and cool. This was a wide-awake alteration of my mental state—a delicate shift of consciousness, without any feeling of disembodiment or disorientation. It seemed a crystallization of my awareness: my mind was singularly focused on the task at hand; the normal, endless chatter of my mind ceased completely. It was an experience I did not take lightly.

The women who accompanied me in the small kitchen area where I prayed encouraged me to continue praying intensely and to further manipulate the mixture in the bowl. When it was agreed that my efforts were sufficient and complete, the *mae-de-santo*[2] took the derecho and put it on a plate, placed the plate on top of the bowl, and brought it into the other room—I am guessing that it was presented to the sacred grove of Egúngún. I was led outside to the porch area where kids were playing, to await more instructions. I had no idea what would come next. I remained very quiet, and the state I had achieved did not leave me. I possessed a remarkably peaceful state of mind—one that I would learn to know again and again in the coming years at the terreiro.

I was next called into the *barracão*—the large ceremonial hall—Oya's house.[3] Oya is the Òrìṣà who is the mother of Egúngún; it is in this *barracão* dedicated to her, that all Egúngún celebrations take place.[4]

Figure 3.1. The entrance to Ọya's house. The red *coluna* or *camieira*, the physical focal point at the center of the barracão, is also known as *ọ̀pá ọ̀run*, the staff of heaven.

In the middle of the room is a red central column (see fig. 3.1), the fundamental spiritual, energetic axis for Babá Égun: "This is where the axé is localized."[5] It is sometimes decorated with flowers or leafy branches. On the right side of the room, chairs had been set up for the men, the same amount on the left side for the women. On the right wall were drums placed in front of the men's seating, and on the front wall of the barracão were the royal thrones, for the Éguns.

Babá Carlos seated me at the front facing the thrones of Babá Égun, sitting Zen next to me for translation. The other women sat on the other side against the wall. This is a typical Candomblé seating arrangement in the barracão.

Though I did not fully perceive it at the time, everything occurred, and it all appeared, as an enormous undertaking and effort to put together. All the members of the terreiro had

Figure 3.2. Inside Ọya's house: the unadorned red *coluna*, the spiritual axis, and the thrones for Egúngún. The back wall is decorated in a forest motif, a visual that provides a familiar environment for the Babá Éguns.

Figure 3.3. Detail of the thrones, or royal seats for the Egúngún in Ọya's barracão.

Figure 3.4. Sacred *atabaques* of the terreiro, the drums are made of wood with calf-skin heads, tuned by a system of cord and pegs. They are called, from large to small: *rum*, *rumpi*, and *lê*.

rearranged their lives to do this work for me, for the spirit of Şàngó Funké, and for Babá Égun. Their faith in their terreiro, their leader Babá Carlos Ojé Dúdú, and Babá Égun, and all the goodwill and love that they represented, was clearly the unspoken motivating force at play. I had no real understanding of what an effort this was at the time. I was trying to go with the flow as events presented themselves, trying to do the right thing by the spirit of my godmother and my own spirit. That the effort of the members of the terreiro was considerable was shown by the amount of people who came out to help. I never felt uncomfortable; I seemed to have been accepted by the group, probably because Carlos's acceptance of me paved the way for group acceptance. I think that I was more of a curiosity to some—a *norteamericano* who spoke not a word of Portuguese, who just *showed up*.

Figure 3.5. Babá Ọ̀lọ́jadé. The patron Égun of Xango Cá Te Espero. Babá Ọ̀lọ́jadé was a ruler in Africa and was specifically brought to Brazil to reside in a house of Xango.

At this point, sitting in the barracão, the women were singing songs—and all were saluting the head Iyalorixá (mother of
Orixá [P], denotes a full priestess)—*Ogum Bonam*—a person
who by the end of my visit treated me like the oldest and dearest
of friends. Babá Carlos explained to me that Ogum Bonam was
such an integral, crucial member that without her they would not

have Òrìṣà initiation ceremonies in the terreiro. Ogum Bonam would become one of my most cherished sisters/mothers in what would become *my terreiro*.

I sat there observing and soaking everything in, not understanding a word of Portuguese or the songs. The feeling that permeated the barracão transcended language, place, and time. I was experiencing for the first time the physical boundaries of the barracão becoming something more—a distinct *other*, a transporting physical environment.

I enjoyed each moment with a unique sense of fascination—comfortably experiencing a version of my tradition on another continent, in a wonderful atmosphere of communal worship, invocation and adoration of the ancestors—an unparalleled event connecting two continents.

Suddenly, the first Egúngún appeared—Babá Ọlọ́jadé—the ruling Babá Égun of the house. Okay, I thought. I had seen and felt many things in my lifetime as an *òlórìṣà* and *babaláwo* with many years of experience, but I was not prepared for the feelings I experienced being in the presence of Babá Ọlọ́jadé. I had not yet been to Yorùbáland, where Egúngún is a more familiar presence, and my previous participation with and knowledge of Egúngún was limited to a brief period in Brooklyn twenty years before. I had dismissed my dream of personal involvement with Egúngún years ago, yet here I was—in the latter part of my life, face to face with something I had thought I would never experience.[6]

> *axé*, Babá Égun, *axé!*[7]
> *axé*, Babá Ọlọ́jadé![8]
> *axé*, Ṣàngó Funké!

I have never felt anything quite like the presence that Babá Ọlọ́jadé radiated throughout the room. It was mirrored by the love and sheer happiness of the devotees, sharing physical communion with their beloved ancestral king.[9] Babá Ọlọ́jadé talked to the people present and particularly called out for some specific persons to impart information to. He then came over and blessed me, saying that Ṣàngó Funké was here (!) and had complimented me. I remain awestruck by the memory. There I was in Brazil, five thousand miles away from home on a lecture tour, and my dead godmother had followed me here and was now communicating and complimenting me through Egúngún—in a terreiro of people I had met only a week ago.

In the far-right corner was the doorway where Babá Égun had entered—as I looked over, I saw what at the time I could only describe as floating flat-panel sheets of cloth. These sheets would appear at the door (and sometimes briefly enter); later I understood them as *aparaká*, or undeveloped Éguns—who are believed to be very powerful and dangerous. (I discuss *aparaká* in chapter 10.) Babá Carlos turned to me and pointed at one of the flat cloth formations, enthusiastically announcing: "Ṣàngó Funké!" My godmother's spirit had followed me to Brazil and now ecstatically manifested in the form of Egúngún, as an aparaká.

Babá Ọ̀lọ́jadé had me kneel in front of him; he blessed my head with his sword—a great blessing, I was told later—I felt its significance the minute it happened. He indicated to me to dance with him. I stepped forward, guided by assistants, "just dance for Babá right there . . ." *I have danced with Egúngún*, I thought. Several Egúngún had manifested by this point. A young man with a stick tapped near the door where different Éguns would seemingly float by. I would later know those male members as *Amuxian* or *Ojé*—depending on rank—and the "stick" as the *ixan* (*işan* [Y]), the spiritually charged branches that control the Éguns and keep them separated from the living. This is the job of the attendants of Égun.[10]

The ceremony continued, then came to a close, and we went back to the porch area where Carlos addressed me and Zen, while we enjoyed a cold beer. He confirmed that Betty had definitely come and needed to be seated as Égun—*assentado*—that is, be given a permanent physical abode for her spirit to rest in. The standard waiting time for a spirit to be considered for seating was seven years, but she had already been dead for many years, so it would not be delayed by any waiting period. It would be best if Babá Carlos and his assistant priests came to the United States, and they would need to do some preparation ceremonies for her.

Babá very matter-of-factly suggested we use one of Betty's bones as a physical essence for the seating. I must have looked surprised, explaining, "Babá, we'll get arrested in the U.S. for that!" We enjoyed the humor of the moment and continued our conversation. This planting of the Gẹ̀lẹ̀dẹ̀, or female Égun, would be different from planting Egúngún, and a female should lead the ceremony.[11] Babá Carlos was entrusted with secrets of the female society, because the last keeper of these secrets was quite old and did not have a female heir. Babá would also have to bring Egúngún to the United States, facilitating the completion of Betty's dream and ambition. (I discuss Gẹ̀lẹ̀dẹ̀ and relate Babá Carlos's story of receiving this knowledge in chapter 13.) He reiterated the importance and necessity of seating her Égun, and that this would bring more possibilities and axé for me.[12]

I was curious and asked Carlos what kind of initiation, or involvement, he saw for me with Egúngún. He exuberantly replied:

"I will make you Ojé!"

Carlos explained that I could come back in September for the first step—which required about three days—and that the second step would come later. I wondered aloud to Babá, "But Babá, maybe it is too late for me . . . and having undergone all these other initiations . . ." He stated emphatically: "Never too late!" I was very moved and surprised to learn not only was the door open for me, but that I could complete the full training and initiation required of an Egúngún priest.

Carlos gave me preliminary *ebos*[13] (in this case, generically meaning preparatory rituals to do at home), explaining that from there I could start the steps to becoming Ọjẹ́. He indicated that three visits were necessary. He reiterated the idea of bringing Egúngún to the United States; he would need to come with some assistants, but all of this was possible.

As we continued our conversation, Carlos stated: "it was you" that Ṣàngó Funké wanted to train in Egúngún. This statement was a shock to me, difficult and emotional for me to grasp, added as it was to the already surreal sense of the day. . . . I was moved and honored, and at the same time started to appreciate both the enormous possibility and responsibility.

We drank beer, smoked cigarettes, and continued our conversation for some hours. I felt privileged to be living this rare life, contented and fulfilled by all I had experienced that day and night, and all the information and blessings imparted to me from the spiritual world. These blessings from Ṣàngó Funké and Babá Ọ̀lọ́jadé had all been made possible by my extraordinary new friend and future godfather in Egúngún, Babá Carlos Ọjẹ́ Dúdú.

As we gathered at the gate to leave, Carlos put his hands on my shoulders, saying in Portuguese: "*Eu já estou com saudades de você . . .*"

"I miss you already."

I continued my journey to Bahia, meeting my other Brazilian goddaughter there, along with some friends from my previous visit. I visited and gave a music class for children at the Pierre Verger Institute. Pierre Verger was a most important researcher, author, and photographer of Afro Brazilian diasporic culture.[14] There I met two people who would become close friends, Beto Bonfim and Hermogenes; they assisted me invaluably in teaching young Brazilian kids how to play drums. Ha! That was no easy feat. But, as I have experienced in almost every country outside the United States, students and people, in general, are so grateful and appreciative for whatever information and knowledge one shares. I also enjoyed a lengthy conversation with Dona Cici, the knowledgeable and kind assistant who works at the Pierre

Verger Institute, who could recite endless stories on the Òrìṣà/ Candomblé tradition. She lives at the terreiro Ilê Axe Opô Aganjú.

I gave a surprise (to me) class at Pracatum, the school founded by Brazilian superstar Carlinhos Brown, and left Brazil with my head spinning—as would've been the case anyway, just from visiting Rio and Bahia—but now with this newfound revelation fueling the course of my life, along with a reserved sense about this new responsibility to the spirit of my godmother and Egúngún.

I stayed in contact with Babá Carlos over the next month. His indication to return in September was ever on my mind—and as the time rolled past I decided to get back as soon as possible. There were considerable funds involved—not so much for the ceremonial derecho, but for the travel. Also, I was working as a university administrator in a very busy music department, and it was perhaps the worst period to take any time off during the academic year. But no matter: this was the opportunity of my life and there was no way I would not take advantage of it. I told my boss I had an emergency and flew to Brazil for an extended weekend, to accomplish what I had set out to do.

SEPTEMBER 2007

Arriving in Brazil on Friday, September 7—the day before I needed to be at the terreiro—I headed to my hotel in Barra da Tijuca. I didn't know my way around Rio yet; I ended up there because of its proximity to the terreiro and it was reasonable and very comfortable. I was eager to start my steps to becoming Ojé, to progress in my elevation, and to take care of the spirit of Ṣàngó Funké.

Arriving as instructed just past 8 a.m. Saturday morning, I had no expectation or knowledge of what kind of ceremony I would be going through. After a ceremonial abô (a bath of sacred leaves) and changing into white clothes—I had a long sit-and-wait for further instructions. Luckily, one of the goddaughters, Veronica, spoke English—so when she was around I could at least have some conversation. (I did not have the advantage of my goddaughter Zen being present to translate.) Otherwise, I was *completely* lost. But, I was there. I was told to rest in the afternoon, as the "party" for the Éguns would start later—the "party" meaning the celebratory drumming for the Éguns to be called to be amongst the living; to be honored, consulted, and venerated.

Around 10 p.m. we all entered the barracão, Oya's house. The drumming started and the magnificent Babá Éguns appeared. I was once again overwhelmed by this experience. I must have looked lost, as author Ailton Benedito de Sousa and his daughter Luciana, a professor, said hello and introduced themselves. They expressed concern that it looked like I was more or less left on my own. They were longtime members of the terreiro attending this annual festival.[15] They both spoke English and accompanied me, doing their best to offer explanations of the events and participants. At that time, I also met Carlos's daughter Karla, who also spoke English. During the drumming when I was addressed—the gravelly voice of Babá Égun calling my initiatory Ifá name, Adetunde,[16] I had to learn the appropriate response: "*A bençao meu paî*" (Bless me, my father).

Around 2 or 3 a.m., after many hours of drumming, singing, and fantastic displays of different Egúngún, we had a break. I thought, "Okay, this must be over soon." I was starting to fade; the high decibel level of the drumming and singing bouncing off the flat concrete walls (I already had a drummer's hearing loss), the traveling, and the disorientation of language challenges were beginning to affect me. All this combined with the general intensity of the room's activities caused a sense of exhaustion to set in.

But it was only another break. The festival was open to the community, and there were maybe seventy-five or eighty people, now eating or having coffee or soda, or a cigarette. During the next segment of the drumming, somewhere around 3 or 4 a.m., I started to question my intentions and myself—*why had I come?* and so on—and thought I really had gotten in over my head. *I have already had many spiritual initiations,* I thought; I should be happy with those. Why did I reach so far out of my realm? I worried that my family and friends regarded me as nuts to fly to Brazil for only a weekend. I am certain they did.

At a point, one of the Babá Éguns got really agitated, saying "There are those here who think I am not real and I will prove that I am! . . ." I thought: Oh man—by that point my head was swimming—what's this? Babá Égun threatened to remove his headpiece—very dangerous, *a disaster*—he was that upset by someone's disbelief. Immediately, an Ògún priest became possessed by Ògún (god of war and iron), and rushed over to Babá Égun to calm him, pleading with him not to remove the headpiece. The mythological roles of Òrìṣà and Egúngún were being played out, their mythic relationship materialized into a real-life drama.

As the sun came up I felt completely exhausted, sitting by myself in the wooden chair in the middle of the barracão. I would be dishonest if I didn't admit this was a challenge for me. But I reflected that progress doesn't come without challenge—sometimes forcing ourselves to weather difficult situations. Things that come easy are valued as such. I dozed off in the chair and then went to look for a place to sleep, now that I thought it was over and people had left.

But as I walked around the corner of the barracão, I saw another Babá Égun outside near the entrance to the *igbàlẹ* (the sacred grove of Egúngún), talking to a small remaining group. It was now around 8:30 in the morning the next day and still the party continued.

I lingered for a while around this Égun, to share this experience, and then turned the corner to the porch area. All sorts of folks were sitting down drinking beer, much to my surprise. "*Oi*

Brian! Quer cerveja?' (Hey Brian! You want a beer?) Ha!—my new friends had serious stamina! Most of the outside visitors had left, leaving about twenty folks socializing over a morning beer.

At this point Cintia, Carlos's wife invited me upstairs to a tiled landing in front of the entrance of the private area of their home. She gave me a straw mat and a pillow, inviting me to get some sleep. (One of the best rests of my life was on this hard, tile floor.) My mind had completely reversed; the feeling of being lost and overwhelmed—thinking I had really overstepped my bounds and tried to grab too much by coming to Brazil—changed to feeling completely at home and comfortable. Cintia's small kindness and some good sleep refreshed me. Now, as I descended the stairs, I was back to myself and headed down for some food and whatever little conversation I could engage between my broken Spanish, English, and guessing at Portuguese.

Soon we were all instructed to go into the barracão—as Babá Égun was to reappear. I realized later that, during the four days I was there (and as I would later understand was typical), Egúngún had the run of the place night and day, and their appearance often required us to gather in the barracão. There was no linear time element present—only a loose sequential patterning of events, on the broadest of scales. I could understand this musically in the same way that John Coltrane scholar Salim Washington speaks of Coltrane functioning in "spiritual time" when he would solo over long extended modal vamps, removing the boundaries of steady chord changes. I likened the night-becoming-day ceremonies to those extended spiritual-time 'Trane solos.[17] This freedom from linear clock time and thinking contributed to our overall state of mind; we were now collectively functioning in spiritual time. This all added to the dreamlike flow of events. Robert Voeks captures this well in his description of a terreiro in his terrific book, *Sacred Leaves of Candomblé*: "There is an indescribable sense of having entered a different world, a reality out of phase in time and space with the bustle and blare on the street."[18]

Egúngún rules the day and the night, coming and going as he pleases—guided only by the Ojé and Amuxian.

We entered the barracão. Babá Carlos, who sat next to me, turned and said: "Ah, I see now that your spirit has calmed down." That was certainly true, and my normal state of calm and general well-being had returned, amplified even. All the doubts brought on by unfamiliarity and exhaustion were erased, as the deeper truth of why I was there, and how my destiny was to unfold blossomed inside of me.

Babá Ọlọ́jadé called me before him and, after blessing me, gave me my title in Egúngún as a member of Xango Cá Te Espero. After he repeated it three times I was "knighted," if you will, into this great terreiro of Egúngún. "Oluwo Pássoro, Oluwo Pássoro, Oluwo Pássoro." I know that no human being gave me this title; being crowned by Babá Ọlọ́jadé, in his otherworldly communication, was one of the great moments of my life. Babá Carlos relayed to me what Babá Ọlọ́jadé was saying: *that he and Ṣàngó Funké were very happy I had made this effort and accomplishment.* Oluwo Pássoro, I later found out, was a title signifying a guardian of Oxalá [P], Ọbàtálá [Y], a symbol of Oxalafon and all things of *Orixa funfun* [P], the Òrìṣà of whiteness and purity.[19] I must carry this honor well.

I was invited to spend the night and Babá Carlos expressed the hope that I would be back the next day, as they were to call Ṣàngó Funké's spirit then. Due to the language barrier I had not understood this previously, and had scheduled a flight to arrive home by Tuesday morning—whereupon I would head straight to work.

Regrettably, I had to miss the following day's events to return home to my busy New York City life, occupied with obligations of a high-pressure job, family, Ifá studies, and music. I had no idea when I would be able to return to Brazil.

Chapter 4

DIARY 3 2008–2012

Obrigação

OCTOBER 2008

The annual festivals for Egúngún occur in the different months of
the year: September for *Babá Ọ̀lọ́jadẹ́,* October for *Babá Adêomim,*
February for *Babá Eyéile,* and July for *Babá Iaô.* I had to plan
around these dates for my next *obrigação* leading to initiation.
Obrigação literally means obligation, a generic term for rituals and
ceremonial offerings. As the academic semester starts in February,
that month would prove impossible, so the next feasible time
was the fall of 2008, October being a relatively slow administra-
tive period at the college. As my trips were always bolstered by
funds from professional development grants, I was usually able to
combine several lectures along with at least a minimal stay at my
terreiro. Otherwise the costs of traveling to Brazil were prohibitive.
I had lecture invitations, and though I was approved for a grant
for this next trip it ultimately never came through, a big disap-
pointment and financial loss. I had already accepted invitations
from universities in Bahia and Rio de Janeiro and had scheduled
my next ceremony—my obrigação—at the terreiro. Determined, I
forged ahead and took out a substantial loan, never regretting the
money spent in these endeavors or the financial burden it incurred.

Figure 4.1. The *roncó,* the small initiate's room where I would stay in ceremonial seclusion and for sleeping. It was also a general room for other male members to leave their belongings and changes of clothes, and sleep.

My first visit in an official ceremonial capacity resulted in my receiving a title within the terreiro. This next ceremony would be more extensive, requiring that I stay for four days at the terreiro, a more formal obligation and the first of three major steps to becoming an Ojé.

The ceremony was scheduled to start on October 18, my natal birthday—a beautiful confluence of events. Arriving in Rio a few days beforehand, I met my workshop obligations at the Universidade Federal do Rio de Janeiro, and was also able to see some friends—allowing me a few days to wind down from the pressures of New York.

Leaving early on the hour-long cab ride from Santa Teresa—a wonderfully hip neighborhood situated high in the hills overlooking downtown Rio—I arrived dressed in white at the terreiro in Jacarepaguá at 7 a.m. on the 18th. Work was already in full swing among the terreiro members. I was ushered to the *iaô* (ìyàwó [Y]) room (*iaô* means new initiate),[1] the *roncó*, where I would be staying, a small, freshly painted white concrete room with a slatted metal window and a couch on the far wall.

During this time only terreiro members were in attendance, no outside community. I rested a bit, and was given some food and coffee. Babá Egún was already present and roaming the grounds. I showered and took an *abô*, the ceremonial herbal bath, dressing in fresh white clothes.[2] After resting for a few hours I was woken by Carlos. With great joy, I embraced my dear friend, ritual brother, and godfather, whom I had not seen in a year. Carlos is an impossibly kind and joyful person.

My part of the ceremony was starting, so we went together and first fed the Exú (Èṣù [Y], messenger and opener of roads) of the terreiro.[3] Carlos proceeded to divine with Exú, using *obì kòla*, splitting one half of the two-segmented *obì* with his knife to obtain the four pieces necessary for divination.[4] He informed me that Exú indicated our offering was acceptable and *irê*, a Yorùbá term for good fortune.

Everything Carlos does is derived from the African tradition, even though he lives on a different continent. We then went to feed *Onílẹ̀*, the female Òrìṣà of the earth. Onílẹ̀ is an Òrìṣà crucial to Egúngún worship; as *mother earth*, she receives the spirits of those who have departed, returning them to her womb.

We were now standing next to Onílẹ̀, just outside of the *ìgbàlẹ̀*—the sacred Egúngún grove whose entrance is forbidden except by Amuxian and Ojé. Several animals were needed to complete my obrigação to Oya, the mother of Egúngún. Babá blessed my forehead and crown with the different birds, and then the back of my neck, and then repeated this with a pigeon.

We were still outside. It was misting slightly, which seemed to produce a light veil in the air. I stepped back against the wall of the barracão under a small overhang of the roof of Oya's house,

Figure 4.2. The Exú of the terreiro. This Exú lives in his own house; he is the Òrìṣà that is consulted first before any ritual activity is to take place.

Figure 4.3. *Oníle̩*, the Òrìṣà of the earth; Mother earth. *Oníle̩* is the fundamental, collective representation of the ancestors. It is here that that *ixan* of the *Amuxian* are mystically charged before ceremonies.

Figure 4.4. The *ìgbàlẹ,* sacred grove of Egúngún; only initiates are permitted to enter this grove.

and entered into a trancelike state—heavy and deep, yet fully conscious, not like the kind of ecstatic trance one might experience as a horse for Òrìṣà or a medium of *espiritismo.* I entered this state naturally and comfortably; I had no idea it was coming. I stood there for many minutes, eyes wide open, peering out through the gentle rain into the grove of greenery—appreciating the calm simplicity of the moment. I received this great gift of clarity and peace. All doubts, fears, and questions of my rambling mind ceased, and my efforts, based on my faith and guidance from the spiritual world, were confirmed. After the completion of this part of the obrigação, we all went into the barracão to sing praises to Egúngún; the drumming was spirited and virtuosic, the group singing full of life.[5]

A goat was brought inside the barracão and several birds were laid out on a red cloth in front of the area in front of the Egúns' thrones. The goat was for everyone present and the Égun Àgbà

Figure 4.5. Drummers of the terreiro. All the young men play; their level of skill is remarkable.

Adêomim (Égun Àgbà is an elder Égun) grabbed it at the door and took it out. I saw the goat hanging from a tree after. In traditional manner—in the same way an animal is used on a farm—every part of this goat would be used—everyone eats and all parts are put to use. Waste is not tolerated, a sin in Candomblé/Egúngún practice. The women picked up other offerings of fruit and various other foods of Egúngún and handed them to the Ojés, who presumably took them to the ìgbàlẹ.

I was instructed to put on a white cap, so my head would not be exposed to the rain, and to return to my room, the roncó. I slept in the chair, and was woken and given more food. I wrote in my diary and then slept again, was awakened by my god-brother, and instructed to first bathe normally and then to take a ceremonial bath of Ọbàtálá. My godmother representing me in Egúngún—Lenira, an *equedi*[6] of Ọya—first helped me clean my head.

I bathed and showered, and stepped outside the bathroom. One of my godbrothers lifted the pail containing the ceremonial bath of Ọbàtálá and ritually presented it to me, then instructed me to take the rest of the bath. I did so, and changed into another set of fresh white clothes. An aparaká appeared suddenly between the area of the bathroom and the roncó, so we had to wait, as one must take great care around an aparaká; as soon as it was clear he snuck me back into the room.

Éguns have the run of the terreiro; it is us, the living, who must watch out for them during Egúngún celebrations. For this is their time here, to be present once again on earth—aiê, the material world of the living—and they are given the run of the house, so to speak. I went to put on a green hat, color coded for Ọ̀rúnmìlà, but was instructed to wear the white hat I'd had on before. I was also instructed that inside my room it was fine not to wear a hat, but that I must never venture outside without covering my head in white. I relaxed and wrote in my diary in the seclusion of the roncó. People came and went—several of the young men left their bags with their clothes to change into later, as this room had a communal purpose. Lots of activity surrounded me while I remained still. I was told to rest well, for the party would not begin until around 10 p.m. Everyone was getting ready and dressing themselves in their finest white religious clothes.

It was now Saturday night (my birthday). We entered the barracão and I was instructed to sit in the front row in one of the rattan chairs. Since a large community of outsiders was in attendance, many additional white metal folding chairs were set up, with a few of the rattan chairs in the front area facing the Éguns' thrones. Drummers were playing full sets of Òrìṣà songs and the women were dancing in the typical Candomblé slow circular manner around the *coluna* in the middle of the barracão, the spiritual axis of the barracão.[7]

Members were saluting each other according to elder status, either by full *doable* (full prostration) or kneeling and offering both hands with the salutation, *motumba axé*, a phrase of respect

Figure 4.6. The women of the terreiro; Babá Carlos is in background leading the attendees in the call-and-response songs. The *coluna* is now decorated with flowers dedicated to Egúngún.

Figure 4.7. Babá Àlejò, "a visitor." Baba Alejo has a simpler manner of dress than the elder Babá Éguns.

and acknowledgment to salute the elders. Offerings were laid out in the area in front of the thrones. Soon the Éguns started to appear. First three different aparaká, then the Babá Éguns appeared. The aparaká, undeveloped Éguns, are considered dangerous, as they are wild in nature, unsettled. Of the Babá Éguns, I was able to identify *Babá Adêomim* (whose clothing is a brilliant blue with gold designs). The next Égun was clothed in a relatively simple flowered cloth—*Babá Âlejô*.

Various Éguns blessed me and crowned my head with the tap of a sword. Since the attendees were separated by gender with Veronica on the opposite side, I had no interpreter and understood little other than someone saying my name (I was now "Oluwo Pássoro" to Babá Égun and Babá Carlos—"Brian" to others). With a tap on the shoulder and a gesture, I more or less understood what I was supposed to do.

Around 1:30 a.m. we took a break—bathroom, stretch, and Guaraná soda pop, coffee, cigarettes, and pastries filled with a delicious meat. I stayed in the kitchen. "It is safer!" Veronica told me.

After the break, we reentered the barracão, the drumming and celebration continuing for another two hours. It was now around 4 a.m. I must have looked like I was drifting, even with the drums roaring and the communal singing echoing off the concrete walls; they told me: "Don't close your eyes!" Okay, I will not. Another break. Coffee, and this time sausages on rolls. My stamina was not on par with that of my hosts. I was experiencing a certain detachment from the events, even though I was right in the middle of them. I'm sure I would have been more energized had I more understanding of the ritual protocol or the songs so I could participate—or understood the language so I could communicate. I had worked many all-night ceremonies of Òrìsà and Ifá back home; the idea of working or participating through the night was not difficult or foreign to me. But I had been participating since 7 a.m.; now I knew to take it to heart when told to get some rest.

Later Ọya, Ṣàngó, and another Òrìṣà came down—"mounted" their priests or priestesses—their presence blessing those gathered.[8] I had not yet understood that Òrìṣà and Egúngún could come down in the same night.

Ọya saluted and embraced Ogum Bonam, the female elder in charge of all things concerning Òrìṣà at the terreiro. It was a beautiful moment, witnessing the love between this celestial being and the elder *mae-de-santo* (mother of the saint). Ọya is the Òrìṣà of utmost importance concerning Egúngún—she is Egúngún's mother. She has nine roads or paths, five of them dedicated to Egúngún. (I discuss Ọya in chapter 11). After saluting the terreiro's elder, Ọya singled me out immediately and embraced me. Without vanity I simply state that this Òrìṣà acknowledged me next. This recognition confirmed and illuminated the transcendent nature of Òrìṣà tradition. I was five thousand miles from home, a complete stranger, yet these immortal beings recognized and acknowledged their son and his intentions, his faith.

The Egúngún Babá Omiloya stood in front of me, trying to communicate something to me. With the help of my brothers miming instructions I finally got it: I should look at Ọya directly while everyone else was instructed to close their eyes. I followed their instructions, thinking perhaps that I was meant to ask Ọya for some blessing, or something, but no one could explain (Veronica, my only interpreter, was on the other side of the room). I briefly wondered if I had not understood what Babá Omiloya and Ọya were trying to communicate to me, but I just relaxed and allowed the experience to happen. I found out the next day; it was simple: Babá Omiloya had me look at Ọya so she could show me something just for me to see and no one else, that was it. A great blessing!

The sun had now been up for an hour and I told my Ojé brother that I needed to sleep. *Ta bom, sem problema.* It was now early Sunday morning, around 6:30 a.m. I was led back to the roncó, where I crashed, waking up intermittently to the drumming, which went on for another two hours. I slept until 12:30, showered, and dressed in fresh clothes. Two or three other young men were asleep on the floor, while I gratefully had the couch. I went back to sleep again until 3:30 p.m. After sending off a few quick texts home, I asked for some coffee and a sandwich, the delicious home-brewed Brazilian coffee providing a welcome boost.

I reviewed the many pictures I had taken the previous night. I was very surprised that taking pictures had not been a problem, although a few times someone had touched my arm at a particular moment and said, "No pictures." Because it had been a public celebration, folks visiting had cell phone cameras out and were snapping away—particularly on the women's side of the room. Babá Égun did not seem to mind. However, should a cell phone ring, he would lunge at that person, furious! The tinny blare of modern technology inflicting itself into the sacred space of Egúngún was untenable.

A little while later I was asked if I wanted more food, and accepted. This time a huge plate of food arrived, and I assumed it was the food of the obrigação. As is typical in the Òrìṣà tradition, all animals shared with Òrìṣà are eaten. Ogum Bonam came for a visit and confirmed—yes, this was the food of the obrigação. Having been shared with the Òrìṣà, the food is no longer mere sustenance, it is a communion. It has elevating, healing, and protective properties. I ate as much as I could; it was an enormous plate of food. Afterward, my face and body both grew hot as I felt warmth spread through my body.

It was Sunday evening. We returned to the barracão as the drumming and singing to Egúngún resumed. I was able to take a lot of pictures, recognizing this rare opportunity to document as much as I could while trying to balance my presence as a participant—not as an outsider taking pictures. This was my family; it was much more important to maintain correct posture and protocol.

Figure 4.8. Babá Ọ̀lọ́jadé transmitting *aṣe*. The front lappets billow out back and forth, moving the sanctified air to the fortunate recipient.

I was very relaxed in spirit now, comfortable, with a great sense of belonging and quietude. Babá Ọ̀lọ́jadé arrived and blessed me, talking to and blessing everyone. At this point my intent to become an Ojé was to be ceremonially confirmed. I sat in a chair sided by both of my godmothers in Egúngún, Lenira and Veronica. Normally Lenira and a male member would have sat on either side of me, representing me, but since only Veronica spoke English in the terreiro, both godmother and godfather in this case were represented by females.

Babá spoke to me, telling me he was very, very pleased I was "spending my birthday in his house"—noting the many blessings for me from Oxalá, Babá Òrúnmìlà, and Babá Égun. He called my name three times to confirm my title and each time I answered: "Awo!" I stood up the third time he called my name and my ceremony was thereby confirmed. Everybody applauded this moment and I danced in front of Babá Ọlọjadé who blessed me with axé from his billowing red and gold embroidered *àpá* panels of empowerment, the invisible movement of the air carrying the axé of the immortals.[9] Then everyone lined up and hugged me (um *abraço grande*), and I saluted the mae-de-santos in the traditional manner of kissing their hands, and they kissed mine. I was very content and took more pictures as the evening came to a close. I was formally permitted to take many pictures now. Later, we sat outside the barracào with a sandwich and a soda and talked to Babá Carlos, who enjoined me: "You will combine life with death with Òrúnmìlà and Egúngún." This was no small statement. We discussed my return in June to study, Babá agreeing that I needed to spend more time at the terreiro to study. These trips had been wonderful and fruitful, but my time was always constrained by work responsibilities back home. The festival for Ṣàngó was to be in late June.

Not for the first or last time, as much as I felt part of a new family, I felt an aloneness on my course here—coming to grips with the fact that though I was operating on feeling and intellectual and spiritual curiosity, it was mostly faith alone. No organized course of study was available on this path; I had thrown all that thinking to the wind. I was in a completely experiential paradigm, with no counterpart back home in the States, no one to consult or talk things over with; and the language barrier was a huge challenge. I knew I needed to spend considerable time here, and learn the language. These thoughts were offset by the deep tranquility and peace of mind I felt. This feeling had brought me here and still brings me back—a deep sense of spiritual love and contentment that overshadows other concerns. Otherwise, why pursue this? I wondered at the Òrìṣàs' plan, and hoped I was doing my best to fulfill my destiny, and to be a good representative of Ọbàtálá, Ọ̀rúnmìlà, and Egúngún.

I returned to my little room, looking forward to a good rest on my couch. My room was a general dressing/nap/hangout room, and sometimes there would also be several young men of the terreiro sleeping there on the floor. Picture this: middle-aged guy on the couch and five or six young men sprawled on the floor in this tiny room, lined up all the way to the door, knapsacks, clothes, and sneakers in every corner. The full fluorescent light was on because sleeping in the dark is taboo during Egúngún ceremonies, and a chair was wedged against the door, presumably to prevent anyone going out during the night, when Babá Égun roams freely.

In the middle of the night I was startled by the sound of a huge bang on the wall next to my couch—the equivalent no less than that of a sledgehammer. No one else seemed to stir but it made me jump. This bang was followed by the gravelly voice of Babá Égun. Our room was next to ìgbàlẹ, the sacred Égun grove; I tried to ignore the noise and turn over, now with my back to the door. The window of the room was made of metal grating and some thin bars. All of a sudden I heard a high-pitched moan and a banging now on the door—really loud—no more than ten feet from my couch. Then again, twice. I started laughing nervously. Next, I heard the window grating slide open and the bars on the window rattled and shook loudly. I got up the nerve to turn over—and there was an Égun at the window looking in—Babá Àlejò! I found out the next day that the reason the door had been wedged closed was not to prevent me from exiting but to keep the Éguns from getting in. Veronica reiterated the next day: the night belongs to Egúngún.

The remainder of the night passed without incident, and the next day was relaxed as people came by my room to say hello, including two of my new sisters, Ọya Tobi and Fabiana. Veronica brought me some breakfast and I told the long story of Ṣàngó Funké and Egúngún in New York, and a bit about my own involvement in the religion. I related to Veronica the whole story of coming to Xango Cá Te Espero, and we discussed Égun, Òrìṣà, and Brooklyn, and how the Òrìṣà religion works in the United States. In the midst of our conversation, the beautiful Egúngún Babá Àlejò once again came to the door, and waved axé to us with his garment. If there is a more dreamlike place, I have not been there. I spent the rest of the day in my room.

In the afternoon, around 2:30, my godbrother brought in plates of food—the food from the obrigação. Referring to the plate, Veronica told me, "Do the best you can." Some of the foods on the plate were unusual; parts of the animals involved in the obrigação are not normally found on a dinner plate. The food was replete with aṣe, which further connects the person to the Òrìṣà or Égun; certain parts of the animal are teeming with life energy and are intended for the persons involved in the ceremony. This food provides long-lasting spiritual and health protection. I ate to my contentment, not really sure of what I was eating, but bolstered by a psychically refreshing glass of Coca-Cola to wash it down—a grand juxtaposition! Coca-Cola or not, a feeling of tremendous warmth spread through my body after I finished eating the sacred obrigação meal.

It was now 3 p.m. Veronica and I reviewed my pictures of the various Éguns and also the different Ojés, Amuxians, and the priestesses and priests of the terreiro. As she went through all the different Egúngún pictures and named all the different Éguns, I was amazed that she knew every single one. I took copious notes so I could later correctly match the names. She even recognized one Babá Égun in another Égun's clothes because his outfit was in repair. I again reflected on my good fortune at being allowed to take these astonishing photos. (In New York City, no one was allowed to take pictures of anything as I was coming up in the religion; secrecy was everything. But that was another time and place.) We finished reviewing the photos and I was once again left to my seclusion.

While I was relaxing and reading alone in the ronco, listening to the Cuban singer Merceditas Valdes, an Égun Àgbà (elder Égun—"the ancient ones")[10] opened the door and stood in the entranceway, moving back and forth, the àpá panels swinging out delivering aşe to me. The Babá Éguns are the embodiment of death; we are warned to never touch them. And though that thought coursed briefly through my mind, it left as fast as it came; my perception shifted to an inexpressible place. Time seemed to stop. How do I explain this dreamlike shift? It was not dramatic and yet it was, as if I were in a room with normal light and then suddenly the light turns blue. I am still in the room, everything is the same, yet not the same. A visual analogy is not sufficient; it is more than that, it's a visceral shift of one's perception of reality.

Even though this lasted no more than a minute or two—to be face to face with Egúngún, one-on-one, with no minders or accompaniment, transported me into their realm—a subtle but decisive, unquestionable shift in consciousness filled me with quiet. Time felt suspended, where a minute may seem like an hour or two—or forever. I was clearly in their world, yet in my world at the same time. Despite the skeptical response one might receive describing an event like this, no one can ever take the truth of it from one who has experienced it.[11] This leads me to wonder if we are always in both worlds simultaneously, and simply do not recognize the fact—but the Egúngún do. Through the Egúngún society, their ceremonies and spiritual wisdom, we for a time contravene the wall between life and death, living and dead, and are allowed to be miraculously in the latter's presence. As my godfather Ojé Dúdú said, *maravilhoso, muito lindo*, so beautiful.

Yet this was *death*, I reminded myself, normally associated with all things negative, at least in Western European thinking.

So why did I feel so full ("all filled up," as they say in churches of the southern United States), content beyond all levels of contentment? Egúngún's primary focus, its tradition, involves communing with the other world. This relationship, and all the preparation, commitment and ritual it entails, contradicts or rejects the perception of negativity associated with death in industrialized countries. Just as heat could be destructive and comforting at the same time, so it is with the spiritual radiation provided by Egúngún, which can provide a great spiritual comfort and uplift from something we normally fear.

At 7 p.m. we all went outside in front of the house of Egúngún. Babá Égun spoke, then greeted us one by one. Ojé Dúdú also spoke with all his godchildren, but as I had no interpreter I did not receive the message being transmitted. I returned to my room. It was the final evening of my stay, and I went through one more ritual *abô*. As I was able to compare the Òrìṣà tradition as practiced in Brazil and New York, I reflected that many of the basic ritual, scientific, and mystical tenets of our religion hold true, no matter the geographical location. This reinforced my notion of a singular, overarching ritualistic and philosophical concept or practice permeating the path of the Òrìṣà, whether it is in Brazil, Yorùbáland, United States, Cuba, or any of the other numerous countries where Òrìṣà worship exists.

When I returned from Brazil, I entered right back into my busy life at the university; I was a full-time administrator with a thousand responsibilities. I felt completely energized, younger, and full of a new certainty about life and my spiritual path as it was unfolding, now incorporating Egúngún. My wife commented on my relaxed and energized demeanor.

One month after my initiation in Brazil I received my first request for a divination session. A woman who asked for a reading came to my home accompanied by her husband, also a follower, and we sat down to consult Ifá. As I cast the *òpèlè* (one of the tools of the Ifá diviner), I happened to glance to my left where the husband sat, and I instantly could see—almost in the fashion of a movie—many things about the husband.[12] Now, it is not unusual that someone comes for a reading and the diviner receives information about the spouse, often important to both parties. This can happen for a variety of reasons. But the clarity with which this happened, and the brevity of the moment, was remarkable to me. I had never experienced such quickness and definition, and thought, "Okay, this is the result of that ceremony." On a subsequent visit to Brazil, I mentioned this moment—where I instantly saw this person's life—to Babá Carlos. He was very pleased and said, "Great, great. That is exactly how it should be." The practical, utilitarian side of my spiritual initiation had revealed itself.

JULY 2010, "A HOUSE OF HAPPINESS"

I was able to visit Brazil again in the summer of 2010, this time with my wife and daughter. After dragging them around Bahia, visiting the beautiful and very old terreiro of *Bate Folha*, they were ready for some "normal" vacation time. Well, good luck with that. I was excited for my family to meet my spiritual family of Babá Carlos and his wife Cintia. It turned out that our last day in Rio de Janeiro was the only time we could get to the terreiro. But it was also the only day we were able to connect with our friend Eve D'Amours, who managed Afro-Reggae, a transformative musical project that grew out of a particularly violent favela, Vigario Geral. Afro-Reggae's sole reason for existence was to steer youth from possible drug-gang involvement. Eve wanted to take us for a second visit (I had been there once before) to the now famous (or infamous, depending your perspective) favela where Afro-Reggae was born and has been developing.[13]

So we spent the entire day with our trip to Vigario Geral, toured their impressive new performance hall and production studios, and arrived back at our hotel hot and exhausted, with the promise of an hour to rest. Then, accompanied by my good friend, the percussionist Beto Bonfim, we were back in the taxi for another grueling hour's drive to Jacarepaguá. My girls are troupers; they endured the long ride and we finally arrived at the terreiro.

We were met with open arms; embraces and introductions followed. As we were talking, Babá Carlos told my wife and daughter they could stay on the terreiro when we came for my next initiations, and jokingly added that I would be confined to my secluded room while they would stay in the comfort of Babá Carlos's house. In his inimitable way Carlos spread his arms and declared: "This is a house of happiness!" Yes, it clearly is.

On this visit, the whole terreiro was very quiet, no activity anywhere. I asked Babá to please let me go to the ìgbàlę and leave a small offering for Babá Ọlọ́jadé. We approached the ìgbàlę. I knelt down in front of the door and prayed for health and all good things, for protection for myself and my family, and all good things for the terreiro. In the middle of the prayer, Babá Égun spoke from behind the door and Babá Carlos interpreted that Babá Ọlọ́jadé was very happy I was here. He encouraged me to continue with my initiation process, saying that he would always bless me and my family.

We resumed our busy lives in New York, but the idea of continuing my initiation in Egúngún was ever present. The logistical challenge of returning to Brazil for the next step was formidable, however, both in getting time away from work and in raising the funds required for travel and an extensive nine-day ceremony.

Without any warning, in March 2012, I experienced a devastating loss in my career. I was faced with having no livelihood, no insurance, no pension; no way to support and feed my family. Amid this ruinous event, I received a phone call from the sister of Terry Winter Owens, a well-known composer I had been close to, and who had passed away a few years earlier from leukemia. I had done extensive work for Terry, commissioning and performing her music and producing her CD, for which I never asked for or received any remuneration. Her sister revealed to me—apologizing for taking so long—that Terry had left me a considerable sum of money.

I was quite taken aback, first because no one had ever given me this kind of reciprocity for my own artistic generosity, and I was very moved. Second, this gift would allow me to fund my next level of Egúngún initiation, almost exactly equaling the substantial ceremonial fees. Amidst my untenable career predicament, faced with unemployment and an uncertain future, I believed this money was destined for me to complete the next step of my Egúngún initiation, especially since it had come unexpectedly from someone who had died three years previously. One could not ask for a clearer inspiration—money from the realm of the dead to pay for initiation into the cult of the ancestors, Egúngún. I cast pragmatic concerns aside and immediately opened a separate bank account and put the money there until I might again travel to Brazil.[14]

Chapter 5

DIARY 4 2013
Amuxian

FEBRUARY/MARCH 2013

As I settled into a new phase in my life—free from the stress and rigors of a high-pressure post in academia—I could now focus on more artistic music projects and in-depth study of Ifá. I had resolved my career situation of 2012 satisfactorily. I was ever aware of a continuing vital purpose of my life: my ongoing involvement with Egúngún. I would soon plan another trip to Brazil to complete the lengthy initiation to become Amuxian (a fully ranked Egúngún priest). This was a significant life goal, and in February 2013 I took an extended trip to Brazil to complete this initiation, and stepped fully into the world of the Egúngún.

As I have stated, Egúngún was always in my spiritual path. Even in the results of my *itá* (the oracle prophecy one receives during initiation into Òrìṣà religion) it was stated: "You must learn *ikú* (death) well." I had no idea what that meant—and no one explained it to me—but I did my best to honor that statement by maintaining a close association with my ancestors as I done for years. I did not realize there would be a path made available to me to further accomplish this goal in the future. Now, armed with resolve, I would take the step of becoming an Egúngún priest. I had already completed my preliminary obrigaçãos to Egúngún; this ceremony would obligate a lifelong commitment.

Amuxian forms the first of two levels of the Egúngún priest-hood. To be an Amuxian is a great honor, achievement, and responsibility. To enter into the cult of Ikú and Egúngún is to establish an intimacy with death, not as a negative force but as a profound reality. I would start my pilgrimage of understanding the mystery of Ikú and its spiritual emissaries—these mystical beings known as Egúngún—whose wisdom is beyond human understanding.[1] For me, this entrance and acceptance was the highest honor. I held the utmost respect for the teachings and was humbled by the faith the terreiro, Babá Carlos, and Babá Égun had in me. Moreover, to be in the cult of Egúngún you must be chosen and approved by Egúngún.[2]

In making my plans for my visit—which would entail nine days of seclusion and ritual—I was in communication with a sister from the terreiro, my sole contact for English-Portuguese communication. We set up dates and resolved as best we could the many questions about necessary items and accommodations before I made the trip. Significantly, we also briefly discussed why a person would go through this initiation. I remember her saying, "All I know is this: Everyone loves the Amuxian; those who go through this ceremony of initiation, well, everybody loves them." I thought, what could be better than that? This statement further buoyed my motivation.

To be initiated is serious business—from all sides. Records are kept of each initiation, recorded and verified by the Associação dos Terreiros de Culto a Babá Égun da Bahia e do Brazil.[3] The society formalizes their initiation of Amuxian and Ojé, keeping records of each one, thus, all ceremonies are witnessed and recorded.

I was aware that participants from other houses, from the centers of Egúngún in Brazil, would participate and witness my Amuxian ceremony. There were Ojé from Ilha Itaparica, Recife, and Rio de Janeiro, representing the three centers of Egúngún worship. It is normal for other priests to be brought in to help with

Figure 5.1. Two *ixans* at rest on the thrones of Egúngún.

the ceremony; this creates an enriched solidarity and assures that wherever initiates might go, they will be recognized and accepted.

The word *Amuxian* means bearer of the *ixan*, or whip, a slender branch specially prepared and used to keep the Egúngún separated from devotees during a festival. All potential Ojé must go through the ceremony of Amuxian first. "Within the hierarchy of the cult, it is the Ojé (highest of the two ranks) who are responsible for invoking the Égun, . . . but only after passing the lower Amuxian initiation level."[4] I explore these subjects in greater detail in subsequent chapters.

In her 1969 article, Dos Santos reveals the necessary steps for consideration for Amuxian initiation and gaining entrance into the cult:

> In Bahia initiation into the cult of *Egúngún* is hereditary in some families. The candidacy of other future *Amúsian* are promoted by some senior *Ọ̀jẹ̀* or a candidate may be chosen by an *Egún*. Finally, special circumstances in the life of a boy or adolescent may oblige the family to have him initiated. . . . In all such cases,

it is only after the vote of the senior *Ọ̀jẹ̀* and the approval of the *Egún*, that the candidate can be initiated.[5]

Dos Santos continues, describing the selective nature of the cult:

It is no easy accomplishment to be accepted and initiated into the *awo*, the secret mystery of the cult. Formerly in Bahia, the more outstanding representatives and those having the deepest knowledge in the *Nàgó* (Yorùbá/Òrìṣà) religion and traditions belonged to the cult. Even today in Bahia to gain entrance into the Egún cult *is a great privilege* obtained through heritage or by personal and relevant merit.[6]

During this period of planning I had a rich dream significant to my next step:

Babá Carlos and I were talking while traveling in a car. We arrived at our destination and entered a building. He led me up some stairs and through an inconspicuous doorway to a room that he clearly wanted to show me. Inside, the room was filled with many Òrìṣàs— the sacred vessels housing the Òrìṣàs' secrets. All were covered in spectacular green and yellow beadwork, the color of beadwork found in Cuban Ifá worship—representing the life-affirming light of the sun and the green miracle of photosynthesis (in West Africa Ifá's colors are green and brown). As these colors are commonly seen in ritual practice, I interpreted the dream as Babá Carlos revealing to me the inclusive nature of his practice of Candomblé and Egúngún with Ifá, as if to say: "No problem, no conflict."

RIO—FEBRUARY

Arriving in Rio de Janeiro on Friday, February 22, I stayed with my percussionist friend Beto Bonfim for a few days, crashing in his living room, then for a few more days at another friend's *pou-*

sada (guest house), appropriately named Casalegre, or "House of Happiness," located in the hills of Rio's premier, funky artistic neighborhood Santa Teresa.

Before going to the terreiro, I caught up with old friends (and met new ones) visiting the house of a fellow musician who drummed for Candomblé ceremonies; became friends and renewed friendships with several of the staff at Casalegre, Ana, Viviane, Pedro, Beto, and Stefano; and was surprised in our conversations how familiar many people were with Òrìṣà and Candomblé.

One person I met, Pedro Oxala (an adopted name indicating he was a son of *Oxalá*), though not deeply committed to Candomblé but inclusive of it in his spiritual vision, described how he had gone through a week-long obrigação—no small thing—for the elevation of his inner consciousness, called ìbọrí. A very spiritual person, Pedro was able to incorporate this ritual into his life, perceiving the fundamental profoundness and spiritual efficacy of the tradition. I mention this so that the reader might have a better sense of the familiarity many Brazilians have with Candomblé and Òrìṣà.

Another person I met, who I assumed would be completely removed from this tradition (i.e., white, intellectual, Western-educated—a classical musician), told me she had gone for a reading with a *mae de santo*, then proudly announced she was a daughter of Qya! Though a topic for another work, the racial, class, and economic constructs within Candomblé seem more fluid than those in the Òrìṣà community in New York City.[7]

After several days of visits, maintaining some music-contracting requirements long distance with New York, and some shopping for additional ceremonial white clothes in the chaotic, bustling section of Rio known as *Saara*—a central-city market—I was eager and anxious to see my family at the terreiro.

By this time my life in New York had stabilized quite a bit, but I was glad I had allowed myself time to slow my pace and reorient myself. When visiting South America (and many other non-European regions) one's sense of time and "on-time-ness" must adjust. In the terreiro, the sense of time operates on a whole other level. Things just seemed to happen, but on occasion I observed others looking askance when I wasn't ready or dressed correctly, as if I should have just *known* that something was about start. Linear thinking or scheduled time is flexible in the world of Òrìṣà and Egúngún, and events seem to revolve around other factors.[8]

After five days in Rio, I took the hour-long cab ride out to Xango Cá Te Espero in Jacarepaguá, with its sprawl, its famous automobile racetrack, and the enormous Coca-Cola factory. I was to arrive on Thursday evening for the start of the initial preparatory ceremony. I was ecstatic to be coming *home*, for no other place in the world gives me quite this feeling of belonging, stability, and overall sense of *rightness* as a human being, or as in my role as an Òrìṣà/Ifá/Egúngún devotee. This ceremony would turn out to be the most profound spiritual experience of my life, while at once the most demanding both physically and mentally. Those demands (which caused disquiet at times) were juxtaposed, however, against the deepest sense of ease, belonging, and tranquility I had ever known. No other experience had provided me with quite this state of being.

I arrived at the terreiro at 4:30, dutifully "on time" to be greeted by Carlos and Cintia's young children Carlos Jr. and Didi (short for Aildés, named after her grandmother). Soon after, Jailson, a.k.a. Mazazi, arrived, who was to be my godfather (Babá Kékeré, literally small, or junior), who, along with my godmother Lenira, would represent me with Egúngún. Then Marlon arrived, and a bit later Fabio; these two great guys were my fellow initiates for the next nine days; we would become the closest of friends.

Though I had been teaching myself basic Portuguese all along, my conversational abilities were still limited, and I had little idea of what was going on or what would be happening later that night—or for that matter, throughout the upcoming nine days. This is no understatement; though I had attended and participated in countless Òrìṣà/Ifá ceremonies, I did not have the advantage of participating in my new terreiro's functions on any kind of regular basis, such as Marlon and Fabio had, and my language skills allowed only the most basic understanding. An initiate to a new ceremony might not have much idea anyway, but this lack of knowing and communication added to my state of mind.

That said, I never had a strong need to know what was going on in this initiation or any other. I always participated on faith; the language barrier, however, did contribute to my isolation, compounding this particular lack of knowing. But my stubborn streak pushed me forward; my determination helped me accomplish a goal that could have been left to languish.

Still, in the afternoon I was hanging out in the porch area, staying out of the blistering, mid-summer February sun, and admitting to myself, honestly and not for the first time, that I wondered what was I doing here—in effect second-guessing my decision. I still cannot fully answer why, on this particular trip and the pending ceremony, I was preoccupied and at times distressed. I reflected on my myriad initiations, more than most people in our practice; I could not surpass Oluwo in Ifá and Òrìṣà; I had already reached that plateau.[9] I had spent a not insubstantial amount of money to accomplish this. I felt I had paid my dues above and beyond, and had nothing left to prove to anyone or myself. But the answer to my unspoken question came: I was on a pilgrimage to complete this part of my destiny, my quest for the knowledge and experience of Egúngún. So, with that resolve, I was ready to move forward.

Babá Carlos and Cintia arrived in their car around 6 p.m. They exude such love and good vibrations that their immediate presence acted like a balm to my spirit. Embraces followed and all the trepidation I had felt fell away, forgotten. I relaxed and felt "home," enjoying everyone's company. Carlos explained that I would be "getting dirty tonight," and I think he said I would be sleeping in the ìyàwó room, the roncó, I had stayed in during my previous obrigação. Definitely, he said, I would be getting *sucio* (dirty!). I told him I understood—80 percent! In hindsight it turns out I had not understood very well at all.

These first two nights were preparatory ceremonies to prepare "the head" to receive the initiation of Egúngún. The first one is an ìbọrí, a blessing and cleansing of one's mind—the *ori* of a person.[10] This strengthens and tempers the mind, readying it to successfully pass through the initiation of Egúngún.

Ogum Bonam, one of the elder priestesses of the terreiro, a shining star of deep feeling and compassion, arrived and gave me a big hug. At 7:30 I was in a deep state of calm and contentment—more so than in a long time—an effect the terreiro has on me and others.

In her best efforts to communicate with me, Cintia was writing and talking at the same time—we had taken to using that method to clarify what she had said if I did not understand. She wrote things down quickly—and I got it! We had found a way to communicate successfully; I was better able to understand the written Portuguese.

Cintia marked my white clothing with a black pen, like I was a kid going off to camp. She wrote on a piece of paper: "putting you in another room with a key" and gave me a key to a small room just inside the house, next to the porch. Going over the clothes with Cintia, she said: "*Tem que estar suade e suja*" ("You are going to be sweaty and dirty"). "Well, okay."

Cintia is the master organizer, plus overseer/wife/mother/disciplinarian. She is full of affection with a nearly constant wicked smile and great sense of humor. She doesn't suffer fools or put up with any nonsense, managing to keep everything together during a ceremony that lasts days and involves scores of people, including members of the terreiro, visiting *Babalorixá, Iyalorixá*, and adherents. Even the general public attends

Figure 5.2. Xango's house, primary altar to Xango. His accoutrements surround him; the crown of the double-headed axe adorns this spectacular throne. A smaller Xango vessel is against the back wall.

Figure 5.3. Xango's house (barracão). Offerings encircle his *pilar*, rose petals numinously carpet the wooden floor.

during the community portion of the festival; her organization skills are no small thing.

The ceremony began with the ìbọrí—a ritual not unlike the rogation found in the Òrìṣà practice in the diaspora, the same purpose of supplication and metaphysical tempering of the head, using different physical materials and gestures.

At this point in my account, I must filter my experience, as I am bound by oaths of secrecy. The details of ceremonies are not public knowledge for good reasons: the realms of mystic knowledge must be learned experientially, and the seeker must make efforts so to appreciate and respect the knowledge of the mystery school, in this case the Egúngún tradition and connections to the ancestral spirits.[11]

Having completed the ìbọrí with my godfather Jailson, who would represent me with Egúngún and be responsible for me, we were led to Ṣàngó's house where we would spend the night—one of the two large barracãos where the large, public ceremonial

Figure 5.4. Vessel of Xango carved from the cajazeira tree by a Bahian artist.
A gift to Aildés.

Figure 5.5. Detail of back wall of Xango's house. The terreiro's moniker and a picture of Aildés, Babá Carlos's mother, adorn the wall.

functions take place. On the way I saw my godmother Lenira; we embraced, and I congratulated her on her new baby.[12] We had mats to sleep on, candles, and multiple vases of white flowers by our heads. At this point we were accompanied only by women, who commenced to sing, beautifully and subtly, as we rested, anticipating sleep and another day tomorrow. It was a beautiful event, a profound passage.[13]

All day Friday I was sequestered in Şàngó's house with Fabio and Marlon, who were going through the initiation with me. Although I had been something of a curiosity to some during previous visits, Marlon and Fabio treated me like a brother. They are just the sweetest cats. One mutual subject we hit upon was Òrìṣà songs. I was surprised when Marlon showed great interest and quoted some Cuban Lukumí songs, found in his studies through the Internet. This was an ideal point of connection; I sang Lukumí praise songs of Ifá to their enjoyment. We also had some big laughs "accusing" Fabio of liking Michael Jackson, playing off assertions of Brazilian machismo, as if this were a crime. No fools, no fun.

We had occasional visitors. Aside from our brief attempts at communication, and trying to rest on thin mats on a hard floor, my isolation caused by the language barrier was stressful. My physical well-being was a concern: to sleep another night on the floor would be nigh impossible; I was dealing with a serious physical limitation this had not been successfully communicated during initial preparations. I had assumed I would then go to the room Cintia had prescribed for me, similar to where I had slept during my first obrigação.

In addition to my physical concerns, I unexpectedly negotiated a difficult time mentally on this day, our second day of initiatory seclusion. I cannot ascribe my state of mind to anything specifically, and I had never experienced anything like it before. I wish I could say I sat through the day unperturbed like some kind of Buddhist monk, but in truth I was troubled, musing upon my death. I would even say I lived through my death in some psychological sense—this was more than an unbidden contemplation on impermanence. These thoughts were unsolicited and unwelcome; I found them distressful and disturbing. Life had already shown me what it meant to face one's own mortality and to intimately consider death. I believe the isolation of the language barrier contributed greatly to my unease on this day. I cannot say if any other Amuxian initiate experienced this, nor do I seek explanation. I cannot remember how long this lasted—I had little time sense other than a fairly long day punctuated by occasional visitors and meals.

I was able to see Ojé Dúdú that morning and with the help of Fabio, who knew more English than I had supposed, explained to Carlos "*não é possível*" ("it's not possible") for me to sleep on the floor. We realized that there had been a significant miscommunication and resolved the situation immediately as he arranged for me to spend the remaining days in a room with a mattress on the floor. Heaven! Luxury! The stress relieved, I could now relax and get ready for the following seven days.

SATURDAY, FEBRUARY 23

After a nice two-hour nap in the afternoon, I prepared for the night's festival, again called a *festa* or party. This started somewhere around 10 p.m. and lasted till 8 or 9 a.m. into the next day. There would be drumming and the procession of the different Éguns, a festival I had witnessed several times. I thought to myself: Ha! I know what I am doing—this is the big public festival for Babá Égun and everyone will dress very nicely. In the past I had only brought the plainest of white clothes, but his time I brought a nice African outfit fitting for an Òrìṣà celebration. I was proud to show I knew what was happening. (Mind you, I had no idea whatsoever when the main ceremony for my initiation would take place.) Cintia came in and said, laughingly, "No, Brian, you are going to get dirty." She asked me to put on the plainest of white clothes. Go with the flow, I resolved to myself.

Part of this ceremony, like any initiation ceremony of African diasporic practice, involves the previously mentioned *abô*, the cleansing, purifying baths of herbs specific to the particular Òrìṣà or entity involved. I took my bath late in the afternoon standing outside of the barracão. The Ojés helped administer the bath—a bucket of herbal liquid over the head—and handed me my simple whites.

I felt I was seventeen again.

This was not like a "Gee, I feel young again!" moment. But rather: "I *am* young again." As I stood there I could feel the essence of my teenage years, the limitless energy, the wide-open plain of my life, a summer day on Woodbury Road in Hicksville, Long Island; the joyous freedom of driving around in my '64

Pontiac—all this memory DNA flooded and blossomed within me. It wasn't like these specific memories passed through my mind like the cliché of one's life flashing before you; it was more the *feeling* of those memories, as when a whiff of an evocative fragrance produces a flash of substantive memory. *I was seventeen* and felt an endless youthful vigor I had long forgotten. And it was not a fleeting moment. I cannot say how long this feeling lasted: I was in the realm of spiritual time where an hour is a day, a day is a lifetime. I felt rejuvenated and relieved of my previous ruminations, which were never to return.

The terreiro is always transformative and healing for me; the cumulative effect of time spent there opened my mind and heart, making me available to all potential experience. I sensed when I set foot in the terreiro that Babá Olojadé was aware of my presence and happy for it, while my own personal Éguns and spirits, those who attend to our individual well-being, bathed in the luminosity of this sacred compound. Thus, a merging of human and spiritual worlds occurs, where the individual integrates psychologically and spiritually with both the unseen forces and with our human initiation brothers and sisters. I view this state of being as part of a group mind, a communal paradigm, where egos and life problems are left behind at the terreiro entrance, allowing a higher and greater purpose. The terreiro environment supports the group mind as a place of repose, safety, and rejuvenation, away from this difficult world.

These ideas were not spoken about. I think the psyche of Candomblé members has no pressing need to articulate such things; their lives are closer to the natural and mystic world, and acknowledge this way of being as an accepted state, not so much as an *other*. The Candomblé members are a very cool (*tutu* [Y]) people; spending lengthy periods among them is transformative, like spending time in a monastery—one emerges changed.

The drumming ceremony/festival for Babá Ọ̀lọ́jadé and all the Babá Éguns began, astonishing in its energy with virtuosic drumming and pageantry: the ecstatic group singing led by the drummers, then spontaneously initiated by both the male and female participants; shouted punctuations of *"iboloribo,"* a rapturous exclamatory signal revealing the participants' joy to these celestial visitors—an over-the-top *Amen,* if you will—an impossibly high level of energy maintained for hours on end; all inspired by the spectacle of the invisible world of ancient ancestral kings made visible, returning from *ọ̀run* (heaven) to *aiê* (earth), whirling in Ọya's cyclonic temperament, brandishing the *irukere* (horsetail fly whip, Ọya's accouterment), the brilliant appliqué *àpá*—the blood red *he-who-defeats-death igbala* panels—fanning out and transmitting "a thousand points of information,"[14] transporting the mystic aṣe of ancient kings.

In the midst of this event—sometime in the middle of the night, surrounded and visited by countless Babá Éguns, in all manner of spectacular cloth assemblages, along with the myriad aparaká—my Amuxian initiation took place.

The deepest, most secretive aspects took place in ìgbàlẹ, the sacred grove outside the barracão. If other writers have chosen to reveal more, I have chosen to limit my description of even the public aspects, reflecting my respect for these rites and belief that these should remain private and experienced.

The ceremony itself was extensive, profound, transcendent. It drew forth visions in me, coming within close proximity to the mysteries of Egúngún and Ikú. When I discussed my experience with Babá, he simply stated: "No one can tell you what to feel or what you might go through."[15]

As promised, my clothes and body got plenty *sucio* "dirty" that night, and around 8 a.m. my brothers cleaned me up as best as possible. As the ceremony drifted into Sunday; it became a day of rest, for me at least. Drumming commenced and continued throughout the day and, as in previous visits, Éguns ruled the roost, roaming freely throughout the terreiro. I had no duties or obligations until later, around 5:30, when I pulled myself together.

When I did wake fully, I remember lying on my mat when a vision of my godmother Ṣàngó Funké came to my conscious mind. She appeared with a huge smile on her face, laughing, resplendent in her bright red, glittering Ṣàngó finery. The message accompanying her presence and her grin was: "*Boy, you really did it, didn't you!*" She was beaming with pride and giddy with happiness as if the smile would burst from her face. That crystal-clear message multiplied my already elevated spirit.[16]

Later that day I mused on another memorable moment: After stepping out of my room, Babá Carlos and I were hanging out in the area adjacent to Oya's house—where all the formal Egúngún ceremonies took place, when a Babá Égun had just turned the corner and come into view. Babá Carlos turned to me with a deeply satisfied look on his face, and, spreading his arms wide as if to embrace the whole terreiro, simply said: "Africa." I was full of respect of Ojé Dúdú's commitment and love for keeping this ancient African tradition alive.

The drumming started earlier on Sunday night—around 6 or 7 p.m.—and I learned this would be a shorter event because people had to work the next day. The drumming initiated the party in the usual manner, with no less enthusiasm or participant involvement. Now there were fewer outside visitors or community members, whose attendance seemed centered on the main party of the previous night. Tonight's attendees were mostly members of the terreiro who had remained all day, along with the visiting priests from the other Egúngún *iles* (houses, terreiros) in Bahia and Recife.

On Monday there was little in particular to do. After an excellent breakfast of fried eggs and coffee, one of my favorite persons, Ogum Bonam, came into my room with her pleasant smile, bearing a huge glass of some kind of fresh fruit shake. We did our best at having a *pidgin* Portuguese conversation, but it hardly mattered—there is a great love between us; she takes care of me and looks at me with a great warmth in her eyes as if she had found a long-lost family member, which I believe in some way I am. The drumming and the festivity lasted late into the evening, with members returning from the community after work.

On Tuesday, Fabio explained to me, "No, no more drumming. Only some ceremonies each night as part of the obligation." That afternoon a truck pulled up and the chairs rented for this event were loaded. Providing rental chairs for over 100 people demonstrated the level of cost involved in putting on such a festival, in addition to paying for transportation for other priests from Bahia and Recife, and the cost of feeding all the guests and community members; this was a huge financial burden for the terreiro to shoulder. This outlay of funds and energy, along with personal dedication and sacrifice, surely benefits the well-being of the terreiro's closest members and families, but also the community at large: initiates, non-initiates, and spectators/curiosity seekers alike.

There were few planned activities on Tuesday, but Ṣàngó and Ọya had other ideas. During the evening a torrential downpour and lightning storm occurred. My sleeping room had a large open window, separated from the elements only by an outdoor porch. Consequently, the wind and rain swept right inside and just about everything got soaked. I have never seen a storm of such ferocity: trees were swaying dangerously, the wind was merciless, and I witnessed the rare phenomenon of lightning balls, small spherical orbs of light accompanying this violent storm and hovering in the air.

After half an hour we were left in total darkness throughout the terreiro. To get out of the storm, a bunch of young neighborhood kids hanging around the yard had piled into my room. The scene was chaotic, but we all tried to keep as dry as possible and keep the water out, relying for navigation on the flashlight from my almost dead mobile phone. Nevertheless, we all got soaked. Only in the middle of the night did the lights come back on.

Wednesday morning found Marlon, Fabio, and myself on our own, as we geared up for the more-or-less uneventful final three days of the obrigação. We made our way over to one of the small rooms that housed a kitchen to make some fried-egg sandwiches. While our presence was required to participate in some type of ceremony each day, we were free to enjoy each other's company as long as we were physically sequestered inside the terreiro walls with our heads covered (in white) while exposed to the serious Brazilian summer sun. During this time together with Fabio and Marlon—doing our best to converse, laughing, eating, and helping me with all the ceremonial aspects—our bond as friends for life was cemented.

The soaking from the night before left me with a pretty severe cold, and by the time I woke from sleep I had missed that day's obrigação ritual, dedicated to the mothers, Ìyàmi Òṣòròngà.[17] I was disappointed, but I knew they were letting me rest.

Later that evening I had long talk with Ojé Dúdú since the now reduced ceremonial obligations allowed for some substantial conversation. Sitting on the narrow platform edge adjacent to the barracão, he spoke of my new obligations as a priest of Egúngún: to be present at funerals and *itutus* (the ceremony for Òrìṣà initiates when they pass), to know the secret signals employed when visiting the cemetery, and many other duties. Babá Carlos complimented me as a great son of Egúngún because of my faith (*fe* [P]). "If Ọbàtálá told you to jump off the building you would." This reminded me of my godmother Betty's comment long ago, when she admonished me over questioning her: "If my godfather (the late *Araba* of Lagos, Fágbèmí Àjànàkú) told me to jump off the bridge, my reply would be: which one?" No questioning . . . just faith.

Carlos and I spoke about future possibilities, including a large obrigação for Ṣàngó Funké in America. Not knowing a word of English, he sounded out *nu-joy-izy* as a place for Ṣàngó Funké's possible *assentado* (ritual seating), not knowing that Betty had always spoken of *New Jersey*—and in fact, is buried there. He remarked that he did not know what he was saying.

Figure 5.6. This is where Babá Carlos and I, and others, talked several times, sitting on the ledge of Oya's house.

Our expansive, if leisurely, conversation gave me both elation and a sense of the seriousness of my new responsibilities. For example, upon the passing of an initiate, I was required to take their possessions, objects or clothes, to the ocean or forest, and so forth. As Amuxian, death now stood next to me, and my life was transformed. And as I had taken this sacred vow, the Éguns who see all would protect me and my family always. While we were talking, an Égun (a *viúva*, the widow) slowly turned the corner, gliding past us at a snail's pace. This Égun was hooded and dressed head to toe in black, with candles in each hand, dispelling the dark. For me, this was representative of death itself. Babá Carlos looked up and said, "Ah, this confirms everything we have been talking about." This confirmation of everything that had occurred meant we had both followed our spirits in good stead, despite the challenging language divide; we had done our best and it had turned out perfectly.

Thursday, the day before I left, I was feeling better but still unwell. Marlon took off his Xango *ilękę* from around his neck and gave it to me. It had a gold *ọṣe* Xango (*ọṣe* is the double-bladed axe of Xango)—that it came from his private use made this gesture personal and special. Later that day I presented Marlon, Fabio, and Cintia with Ifá *ilękę* and *ides* (the necklace and bracelet dedicated to Ifá). When Babá Carlos came into the room I offered him the same; he was also very appreciative.

Friday completed my obligation and later that day I returned to Casalegre to prepare for my journey home.

Chapter 6

DIARY 5 2016

Visiting the Matrix: A Trip to Itaparica

APRIL 8, 2016

It had now been three years since I had been to Brazil. I was traveling with my daughter and we spent a week together on vacation in Rio. She headed back to school in New York while I headed to Bahia. My plan was to visit Itaparica. Itaparica is a small island where the Egúngún society has been maintained since the early 1800s. I relaxed for a few days at a hotel in the Porto da Barra area right near the beach, taking some time out to see my goddaughter and a few friends, and complete a few readings.

I started out for Itaparica, the mecca for Egúngún, in the early morning. Lying just across the bay from São Salvador, Bahia, Isla Itaparica is a small island (fifty-six square miles) reachable only by *launcha*, a small boat, a forty-five-minute crossing of the Baía de Todos os Santos (Bay of All Saints).

I had no idea where I was going—no connections, no names; I thought just to step foot on the island where Egúngún has thrived for two hundred years. My goal was to make my way to Ilê Agboulá (if I could), the founding house from whence my terreiro and others were born. If I was to write about Egúngún, I thought, at minimum I had to feel the earth of Itaparica under my feet, to physically connect with this mythic source.

Figure 6.1. Arriving at Isla Itaparica by small boat, the *launcha*.

Arriving at the landing point of Mar Grande, I wandered around the little town area by the docks, trying to get my bearings in the sweltering sun, as ubiquitous taxi drivers offered their services and tourist information. My research indicated that a general area of the island famous for Egúngún was Ponta da Areia; other than that I had no idea where to go. I grabbed a *stupid-cold* Pepsi and began walking back toward the arrival plaza; when I was approached by yet another taxi driver, I said, "Okay, let's go!"

Fortuitously, my driver, Josemar Itaparica, knew exactly where I wanted to go, and knew members of the temple and community of Ilê Agboulá. We drove into the area of Barro Branco (white clay)[1] where Ilê Agboulá is located, and began climbing an impossibly steep hill in his small, very old car; the road had deep ruts and crevices that would have challenged even a Land Rover. But "*sem problemo!*"; Josemar got us up the hill, even as each rut and bump jolted our spines. Three-quarters of the way up the hill we stopped at a house for information from a lovely

Figure 6.2. Top of the steep, rutted dirt road on the way to find Ilê Agboulá, located a short walk from this point.

Figure 6.3. The outside wall of Ilê Agboulá (house of Agboulá) proclaiming its official cultural designation, the Beneficent Religious and Cultural Association, Society of Egúngún. Omó Agboulá means children of Agboulá. There are two sketches of *aṣọ* Egúngún and a dove, the universal symbol of love, peace, and hope.

woman and her daughter relaxing on their porch. A young man named Marcos came by and said he would fetch the person we needed. Communicating in my *Portugues basico*, their open-hearted reception cut through the language barrier. Marcos returned about twenty minutes later with Ojé Augusto of the temple Ilê Agboulá. I had found my hoped-for destination. We thanked the others for their warm hospitality and began walking down the dirt road, then up another road, and, rounding a bend, through an opening between two large bushes, where in the clearing stood Ilê Agboulá.

I was now standing in front of the most historic Egúngún temple in Brazil. *Exú* (the Òrìṣà that opens doors and makes all things happen) surely had guided my undertaking. He was indeed in full swing, opening roads so I could find my way to the foundation of Egúngún in Brazil.[2]

The day of my arrival on Itaparica coincided with the anniversary of a serious but successful surgery I'd had the previous year. It was indeed a life-affirming and unplanned moment to celebrate that anniversary by setting foot on the island where the cult of Egúngún had been sustained for nearly two centuries. I reflected on Babá Carlos's message to me after my Amuxian initiation: that Egúngún would unceasingly protect and watch over me.

I was introduced to the head Ojé of the temple—Augustine, Bàbá Óluyde. He greeted me and we spoke fondly of Babá Carlos, and the recent initiation of younger Carlos Jr. as full Ojé. Unlocking the outer doors of the terreiro, we entered into the Ilê proper, saluting Exú on our right, then into the barracão, the formal hall for celebrations of Egúngún.

Babá Óluyde encouraged me to have a consultation and make my presence known to greet Babá Egúngún, then and there. I'd not had this in mind at all, but I considered it an auspicious opportunity, and impolite not to, so I agreed. I reminded Augustinho of my limited Portuguese. He looked me in the eye

Figure 6.4. The main hall or barracão of Ilê Agboulá.

and said: "Ah Babá, sem problemo . . ." *C'mon man, it's going to be spiritual communication anyway.* Okay.

We exited the barracão at the opposite end, into the grove behind it, in close proximity to the ìgbàlę, Egúngún's sacred house. On the immediate right was Ògún's tree,[3] and next to that appeared the shrine of Oníłę (mother earth), central to Egúngún worship. Directly behind Oníłę stood the imposing sacred *ìrokò* tree.[4]

The grove exuded a vibrant tranquility, as if thrumming with unheard vibrations. I said my prayers and petitions over the offering I held in my hands, which was then delivered into Babá Égun's ìgbàlę.

After a short time, Babá Ocúnilade appeared. His spectacular clothed assemblage was immediately compelling; it was a dazzling display of aqua, blue, and silver, offset with delicate white finery, constructing a multifaceted aesthetic. The deep visual impact of this Egúngún outfit further beckoned me into the numinous world, representing the presence of *ará ọ̀run*, a visitor from heaven, "people from the life beyond."[5] Only garments such as these are adequate to house the royal personages of Egúngún, sufficient in their splendor to reflect their veiled essence—*power concealed*[6]—at the same time magnifying and multiplying their spiritual authority.

I greeted Babá Ocúnilade in our ritual manner, addressing him with an Egúngún salutation:

Iboloribo!

A bênção meu pai! (Bless me my father!)

He spoke to me in a high, gentle, wavering "voice"—what I call the "other" voice of Egúngún—and blessed me with aṣe by waving the *abala* lappets, conveying blessings through currents of air. He was very pleased that I had come to visit him and the temple of Ilê Agboulá.

Rather than move in any human-like manner, Babá Ocúnilade appeared to glide gently toward me. He spoke with an enigmatic reverberation; his movements seemed embedded in nature, as if the undulation of a forest grove. I could feel an invisible radiance of beneficence and love exuding from him, gifting me with an irrefutable sense of mystic disclosures. Acknowledgment by a Babá Égun is both transportive and transformative.

My brief visit with the glorious Babá Ocúnilade deeply enhanced the magic of my island visit. His parting words were: "*Agboula pede para nao esquecer que veio ao terreiro dele Yes?*" ("Don't ever forget what you have seen here today at his terreiro").

I thanked him and he majestically glided away, returning to his home in the ìgbàlẹ. Babá Óluyde, Babá Augusto, and I had struggled with some translation of the conversation. I didn't want to miss a word, so with the help of the Portuguese translator in my mobile phone—even in the deep "campo" of Itaparica—I was able to parse everything Babá Ocúnilade imparted.

After taking a few pictures, expressing my pleasure and deep gratitude, "*Eu estou muito feliz e afortunado, e muito obrigado,*"

I thanked all the Ojé and members of Ilê Agboulá for receiving me in such a gracious manner.

The next morning, Saturday, found me on the beach at Porto da Barra on the mainland, writing this diary of events. In two days I would return to Rio to complete my obrigação for Babá Ọ̀lọ́jadé.

RIO DE JANEIRO: MEETING EXÚ!

Monday, April 11

I arrived at the terreiro late in the afternoon; not too many other folks were around yet for the evening's activities, but that would soon change. I spoke with Cintia and the kids, catching up in my now slightly improved Portuguese. As more and more people began showing up I realized it would be a very busy night, with Babá Carlos and his godchildren helping many people, completing obrigaçàos, and consulting about various life problems and situations.

It was time for my obrigação and we piled into a car; per instructions, I removed my shoes and belt and all things from my pockets. The purpose of my obrigação was to promote general physical well-being and health. We drove about fifteen minutes to a rocky dirt road leading into an open area spotted with several trees. It wasn't exactly a forest, but we were deeper into nature, further from the modern world. We brought several types of fruits and vegetables as an offering. As I laid each item on the cloth we had spread out on the ground, I was instructed to pray for what I wanted. The vibe started to change as I became more focused, and a strong, deep feeling began to permeate the air, intensifying as I presented the different kinds of fruits and such to the ground. After completing the lengthy prayers, I was abruptly instructed: "Okay, back to the car." We headed back to where it was parked, about thirty feet away.

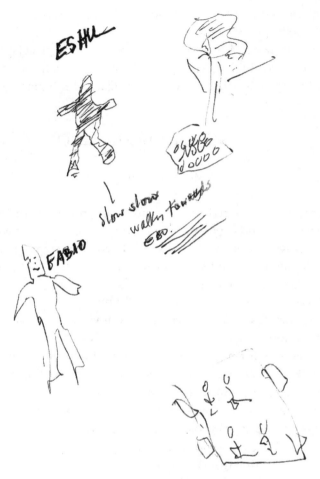

Figure 6.5. Author's sketch of Exú walking to receive his offering.

Sitting in the back with Daniel on my left and another person on my right, the driver had already started the car and Fabio was walking toward us. I looked through the back window and saw someone else moving slowly toward the *ebó* (offering). I got confused and said, "Hey, where are we going to put that person?"

Fabio got in the car and as I turned to Daniel with my question I saw he had a big smile on his face.

Fabio simply said: "Exuuuuú!"

"Whooooooaaaa! *Maravilhoso!*"

"Muito, muito excellente obrigação!"

I asked: "*Isso é normal?* Is that normal for you guys to see Exú like that?"

"Nooooo, just sometimes—very special."

Man, we were all so happy! What a gift, a moment to see Òrìṣà like that, Exu's appearance accepting my petition for vibrant health. This exceptional occurrence caused me to once again reflect on how robust Òrìṣà are here in Brazil.

Later that night, when Babá Égun appeared in the barracào, his first utterance was to me, asking, "How are you feeling; how is your body?"

JUNE 2016: XANGO'S FOGUERA

RIO DE JANEIRO, XANGO CÁ TE ESPERO

Wednesday, June 22, 2016

Upon arriving at the terreiro at 8 p.m. to greet my family, they asked if I could stay for a small Ṣàngó party. Of course! Small meaning "short," four or five hours. So happy to be at my home-away-from-home, I meet and greet Ogum Bonam, who has embraced me since my first days in the terreiro. The festival drumming in Ṣàngó's house is beautiful; participants are mostly members of the terreiro. Ṣàngó possessed several of his children, and I am again struck by how effortlessly the Òrìṣà manifest here in Brazil; there seems to be a clear channel to the heavens.

Drumming and singing to the Òrìṣà is like a call to the heavens, opening a spiritual route for the Òrìṣà to come to earth and manifest in their mediums, a circular appeal of metaphysical rhythmic signals that call and invoke manifestation. My godmother Betty explained that in the United States, this process takes longer than at "home" in Yorùbáland.[7] I believe Brazil has the same "home" status when calling the Òrìṣà, who have been invoked there for nearly two and half centuries. This particular consecrated geographic location, the terreiro of Xango Cá Te Espero, has been active for almost fifty years, and thus has become a spiritually charged base of communications, if you will.

Equedi is a fully initiated priestess with the rank and responsibility to take care of the mediums during the time of possession, when they are taken over by their particular Òrìṣà. Fascinating for me is the intermittent moment of rest and repose for the Òrìṣà during the celebration, when the *equedi*, who are taking care of the Òrìṣà and the mediums, ascertain that a particular medium needs to pause (for lack of a better word). They are led to the side and both hands are raised chest-high with palms outward, a unique suspended position of repose. This high level of discipline by the mediums *and* the Òrìṣà is impressive.

Meanwhile, Babá Carlos sings furiously with a parched throat, looking around the assembled members for a throat lozenge.

Thursday, June 23, 2016

The next night I arrive for Ṣàngó's *foguera*—his bonfire. Thirty-five or so members of the terreiro are assembled along with a few guests. We are outside the barracão next to Égun's ìgbàlẹ, where the young men have built a tremendous bonfire. The care with which the large logs have been crisscrossed results in a stunning *foguera*, a beautiful sight. This is the yearly celebration to Ṣàngó, one of many scheduled annual events celebrating either Òrìṣà or Egúngún.

Speaking with Babá Carlos before the formal activity takes place, he explains apologetically that he has no time for email or to write; he just works, comes home, does Candomblé—shouldering a huge responsibility as head of the terreiro, endlessly helping people—and then sleeps. I tell him *sem problema Babá*, I understand.

The initiated devotees—mostly female—slowly dance in a circle around the bonfire, and different Ṣàngós start to possess their priests and priestesses. Twelve different paths or avatars of Ṣàngó are recognized in Brazil; consequently, there are variations of colors of dress, not limited to the standard fire engine red associated with Xango.[8]

A man about thirty years old sitting next to me is on his phone and wearing jeans—I think (foolishly imposing my ideas of ritual protocol), *"Hmmm, on the phone, not dressed in white..."* Well, fifteen minutes later his Ṣàngó arrives in all his manifested glory, "coming down" powerfully on his "horse."

Ṣàngó is stunning in his presence. The possession transformation is profoundly firm and complete; the presence of the Òrìṣà is strong and radiant as Ṣàngó makes his rounds among the many Ṣàngós who have manifested—*eyes unblinking*, slightly bulged—possessed of the deep spiritual gaze universally manifest in Òrìṣà trance (and recreated in Yorùbá sculpture). His face soaked in sweat, his body electrically ecstatic with energy, as if every gesture is informed by some uncontainable current. He is soon wrapped at the waist with a white and blue cloth to welcome and acknowledge Ṣàngó's presence, the colors identifying his particular road. He is no longer a mortal *with cell phone and jeans*, but now sanctified messenger—absent of the regal traditional dress found in a more formal setting, his street clothes irrelevant to Ṣàngó's will to appear. Energy rolls off him in waves.

Ṣàngó approaches me to salute. I'm honored as he hugs me around the waist, lifting me off the ground, and with his face next to mine urgently grunts an exclamatory salutation.

Words are a faint substitute for the experience of being literally lifted by Òrìṣà, to be embraced, to be in their presence. It is difficult to transmit the feeling one gets witnessing the Òrìṣà, to experience viscerally the transformation as the deity "comes down" in the body of the devotee, a metamorphosis of ecstatic trance. Experiencing this over and over again in Brazil (and in

Africa and the United States), there is no room for rational thought to argue as to the authenticity of the experience.

The practice of the Òrìṣà tradition through Candomblé in Brazil is one of great discipline: the adherents, the mediums, the equedi and the Òrìṣà themselves conform to an extraordinarily strict adherence of ritual protocol. I have seen this on numerous occasions in both Rio and Bahia, and tonight is no exception, as the Òrìṣà continue to acknowledge, salute, and bless the attendees.

Cintia comes over and hugs me, then she catches Ogum Bonam's eye, who walks over and joins in this familial embrace, for no other reason than its own.

On a break, as Fabio is telling me a story, we are summoned to return and sit down on the concrete shelf surrounding Ọya's house. All of a sudden Babá Égun appears, coming out of ìgbàlẹ, his sacred grove. He enters from the gateway of the ìgbàlẹ, and, as always, his appearance is stunning: he arrives bent over—the nature of this particular Babá Égun—in all of his spectacularly draped glory, followed by two aparaká. The initial appearance of Babá Égun always evokes a special response in me.

The visual aspects of this very striking experience inform, edify, and empower the resplendent nature of these immortalized spiritual beings; it is indeed a "feast for the eyes." I am filled with a sense of grace and gratitude being in the company of these materialized souls. Although they represent the dead, they have a celestial quality, far removed from the visitations of dead spirits (*muertos*) that manifested in my early training as a medium at the *mesa blanca* séances in Brooklyn.[9] The Egúngún are deified ancestors of flawless repute from generations ago. In life, their character would have had to have been unassailable, a role model for others. They embody their collective community, fulfilling the role of moral arbiter, necessary to the health of the terreiro, their extended families, and the community. They are people from the life beyond, the dwellers of heaven, the immaculate ones.

PART II

Egúngún:
Custodians of Endless Memory

"They represent a wisdom beyond
all human understanding."[1]

Chapter 7

ANCIENT KINGS EMERGE

Dàrìnnàkò,
Ó dojú àlá,
Ó doko aláwo

Till we meet each other by chance
Till we meet in dreams.
Till we meet in a diviner's place.[1]

The Egúngún society is the ancestral society of the Yorùbá, whose purpose is to make possible the temporary incarnation of honored ancestors—the Egúngún—through specific rituals and festivals. (It is also commonly referred to as *O Culto do Egúngún*—the cult of Egúngún—simply meaning a system of religious veneration, but used less because of the pejorative association with the word *cult*.) They also are commonly known as Égun, Babá Égun, or even simply Babá (father).[2] "According to Babá Carlos the term Egúngún in its simplest definition is "male ancestor."[3] Babá Adewale, a babaláwo from Nigeria, echoes this even more briefly: "ancestor."[4]

It is the societies' function to invoke these honored and immortalized ancestors to once again "share physical fellowship with their relatives on earth."[5] Thus, the word Egúngún generically defines ancestor, but also refers to the ritually prepared, honored spirits who incarnate during ceremonial timespans, and the society of priests who make this possible. In Brazil it is called *Sociadade Egúngún* [P].

Not every ancestor becomes Babá Egúngún, the immortalized and honored spirit; the ancestor who would become Egúngún would have to have led a scrupulous and righteous life, a person of irrefutable character.

Though we can acknowledge that not every ancestor is "ancient" or was a "king" (though many were), they represent the *wisdom* of antiquity and lineages that go back to an unknowable time.[6] Pierre Verger refers to them as "the cult of the ancients."[7] In Brazil, for these materialized spirits of the past, the additional moniker of "king" is common, even a given. They are regal in character and additionally so in their appearance; their magnificent clothing reflects their honored status. Egúngún are treated as kings, whether they were royalty in their lifetime or not. In an earthly acknowledgment of this status, the anterior wall of every barracào is lined with ornate chairs, each representing "a throne or seat of authority."[8] One might hear in my terreiro: "That is my king, Babá Ọ̀lọ́jadé." And they truly are kings; they are humbly venerated and respected, and their word is sacrosanct and unquestionable.[9] When Babá Carlos informed me that my own goddaughter Zenaide was a daughter of Ọya, I asked him: "How did you confirm this, Babá, did you read her with the *buzios* [cowrie shell divination]?"[10] "No. Babá Ọ̀lọ́jadé told us." It was unquestionable.

There are those Egúngún of unknowable age like Babá Olúkọ̀tún, Olórí Égun (the supreme chief of Egúngún), considered by Brazilians to be one of the founders of the Yorùbá people.[11] And Babá Ọ̀lọ́jadé was a king during his lifetime in Africa. His fundamental physical representation, his *assento,* was brought from Africa and now guides and protects the members of our terreiro. This would also be an example of a Babá Egúngún representing a collective, a time period, and a locale, a communal Egúngún whose presence represents his full lineage and that of his past and present community.

Egúngún's faithfulness is to the community, not to a single person. Egúngún helps everybody, and restores and balances social order. P. S. O. Aremu states: "Egúngún worship is one of the ways to stabilize man's world, for traditionally, the worship stands as a bridge between heaven and earth."[12] Babá Égun are acknowledged as sacred beings representing the wisdom of the ancients. And their word is irrefutable—because of this, combined with the adoration of those who perceive them to be divine, compassionate fathers—they enjoy the status of kings and the moniker is apropos.

While Egúngún society comes from Yorùbáland in West Africa, here I focus on its manifestation in Brazil. The people who brought this West African culture to Brazil are called Nàgó. According to anthropologist Renato da Silveira, "*Nàgó* was a generic term used in Africa by neighboring groups to designate Yorùbá-speaking peoples, no matter what ethnic group they belonged to."[13] The Nàgó constitute the "nations" of West Africa that made the greatest cultural impression on Bahia, the carriers of a tradition whose richness was derived from the individual cultures of the different kingdoms of which they were born, in Kétu, Òyó, Ègbádò, and Ègba. The Nàgó brought their traditions and customs, and, as Dos Santos states: ". . . above all else they brought to Brazil their religion."[14]

Although there is a great variety in the manifestations of Egúngún in West Africa itself, as well as in Brazil—the types, the stylistic dress, the specificity of individual family Éguns, and so on—I believe they retain an identical purpose, an identical reason for being. (I discuss the differences and similarities and the idea of African continuity, retention, and evolution in chapter 9.)

The Egúngún cult functions to actively venerate the ancestors. This may be a hard concept to grasp for the average Westerner who associates death with a negative occurrence—an absence, a void—and consider those who have passed on as an entombed, inactive, psychological memory. But in fact, most cultures venerate their ancestors in some form, from the simple leaving of flowers and gifts at a memorialized gravesite, to the Day of the Dead in Mexico, to the monthlong Festival of Hungry Ghosts in Singapore. For the Chinese, veneration of their ancestors is an integral part of their culture, and the Catholic Church is in constant communion with their own Egúngún—the saints (going so far as to possessing a bone of that saint in the reliquary to maintain contact).[15] Throughout Africa, traditional societies historically had fundamental precepts and rituals regarding the veneration of and communication with the dead. From Nigeria, Aremu writes:

> It is possible to have the conception that there is afterlife and that between those who have gone there and those who are still here on earth there is a close and active bond. In the life of every Yorùbá man and woman, worship of these deities (Egúngún) is held in high esteem and special regard is usually given to them, especially by the devotees. Annual visual presentation is usually organized collectively when the spirits of the ancestors share physical fellowship with their relatives on earth.[16]

In both Yorùbáland and Brazil, then, Egúngún is a secret male society charged with the veneration of the ancestors and the responsibility of bringing these ancestors to earth—*ará òrun,* or citizens of heaven—during annual festivals, to temporarily reenter the society of the living, reuniting with their families.[17] They are invoked in determined circumstances and by means of well-defined rituals.[18]

As the Egúngún society is a male society, we see a balancing female complement in Gèlèdè, the female society dedicated to the Ìyá Nlá (The Great Mother). According to Dos Santos, "The working out of the balance between these two poles (of matriarchy and patriarchy) is accomplished by institutions, whose latent and manifest contents permit such an elaboration. In the same way as the masculine ancestors have their institution in the

Egúngún, so have the Ìyàmi (our mothers) their female counter-parts, their own institution in the Gẹ̀lẹ̀dẹ̀ society."[19]

The Gẹ̀lẹ̀dẹ̀ society is dedicated to the divine feminine creative principle as personified by Ìyá Nlá, who "epitomizes the pro-creative power of the female," and reflects the idea that "human beings can relate to one another as children of the same mother."[20] It is within this society that ceremonies are performed for female ancestors who are venerated and immortalized; Margaret Drewal describes the masked performances of the Gẹ̀lẹ̀dẹ̀ "that honor the extraordinary powers of women."[21]

There are several myths describing the original ownership of Egúngún as belonging to women, and various stories of how it came to be owned by men, some whose translation seem to fit a patriarchal mindset.[22] Pierre Verger recounts the Ifá Odù, Ọ̀sá Méjì, which tells the story of women being the "original owner of Egúngún's cloth."[23] It is clear that women are essential and hold important titles within the cult.[24] The female gender has an overar-ching relationship to Egúngún; after all, it was Ọya who gave birth to the nine children, the last of which would become Egúngún.[25] (We reflect on Ọya's defining role in Egúngún in chapter 11.)

Though the word *heaven* is a convenient term to describe the afterlife—and the common-usage translation of ọ̀run (Y)—we must be careful not to confuse the Yorùbá concept of the afterlife with the more simplistic, paradisial Christian concept of heaven. "Ọ̀run is an abstract conception of something infinite, very distant and very large."[26] The Yorùbá have no notion of diametrically opposed heaven and hell. They also do not view heaven as a place of salvation after suffering on earth; rather it is a continuation, a change of address. Ajuwon states: "For the Yorùbá, death is not a finality. It is a gateway to another kind of life."[27]

Ìdòwú describes the afterlife for the Yorùbá thus:

Death is not the end of life. It is only a means whereby the pres-ent earthly existence is changed for another. After death therefore, man passes to a "life beyond," which is called Ẹ̀hìn Ìwa—"After-life." The Ẹ̀hìn Ìwa is of more importance than the present life, however prosperous this one may have been. The Yorùbá thus speak of Ẹ̀hìn Ìwa *ti 's' ẹ́gbọ́n* òni, "After life, which is the superior of Today (the present)."[28]

Their idea of heaven is more like home, thinking that, according to the traditional Yorùbá proverb:

Ayé l'ojà, ọ̀run n' ilé.

The world is a marketplace, heaven (the afterlife) is our home.

Ọ̀run is described in the abstract, as *a place beyond*, a residence in which they will continue their life, and from their new abode they will remain active participants in the family they have left behind.

The history of Egúngún is directly linked to Ọ̀yọ́, and several sources link its origin to Nupeland, home of Ọya, the mother of Egúngún.[29] The Éguns are the great protectors of the people and the community, and function both individually, as part of a family's lineage, but also collectively as corporate entities, which in turn represent full lineages and kingdoms from generations ago. Morton-Williams states: "They [those who have passed on] also know they will become grouped with the ancestral spirits of lineage and town, whose intervention will be invited from time to time by their survivors."[30] The Egúngún offer advice, give individual blessings, shield and shelter their loved ones unequivocally, and their presence is a metaphysical and magical antidote for the ills of the world. They are settlers of disputes and conveyers of titles. Their word is unquestioned and sacro-sanct within the society. According to Lawal: "As the word of the ancestor is law, some Egúngún serve as judges, helping to settle outstanding disputes in the family or community."[31] Perhaps of greatest importance, on the most human level, is the joy they bring to the world, the sheer happiness they bring to the living, who see their grandfather or great-grandfather return, embracing their mutual presence and reciprocal delight, comforted in the knowledge that life continues.

In Brazil, the Egúngún cult has existed on the small island of Itaparica since the early nineteenth century, protected by the isolation of this island home. Itaparica was an island of fisherman with a sparse population, and until the 1970s, except for a few vacation homes, only local inhabitants lived there. Egúngún adapted to Itaparica after being transported from the Kétu area of Yorùbáland during the slave trade. Kétu exists both in present-day Nigeria and the Republic of Benin, divided by the arbitrary border created by Europeans in the Berlin Conference of 1885. (The history of Egúngún on Itaparica island is explored in chapter 12.)

When asked to define the cult of Egúngún, Balbino Daniel de Paula, of Ilé Agboulá on Itaparica, described Egúngún "as the preservation of collective existence. . . . Egúngún worship is the cult of ancestry. It revives the principle of collective existence to keep the ties of kinship between the family and the globe."[32] This idea confirms the ritual performance as an expression of a lived philosophy of shared existence, of living with communal solidarity. Egúngún teaches us to cherish the bonds within our families, as well as our neighbors, our entire community, and all of humanity.

Existing in both the past and present, Egúngún represent the collective of familial and community ancestors and their worshippers. They inspire us to broaden our concept of linear time promoted by the industrialized world, and to expand ideas of communal living and shared existence within our initiation communities, and even to all of humanity.

As described by Thompson, the Egúngún are

Figure 7.1. Babá Adeborun.

Magnificent spirits [that] represent the departed kings, founders,
and leaders of Yorùbáland. These spirits, covered with voluminous and highly valued clothes, are called Egúngún. They incarnate the spirit of the dead. Some come to judge the world. Some
are purely entertainers. Others extend the authority of the elders
to infinity. They represent wisdom beyond all human understanding. Their shapes are otherworldly and very strange. They are
creatures of two worlds.[33]

Figure 7.2. Babá Adeborun.

Figure 7.3. Babá Adêomim.

Figure 7.4. Babá Adêomim.

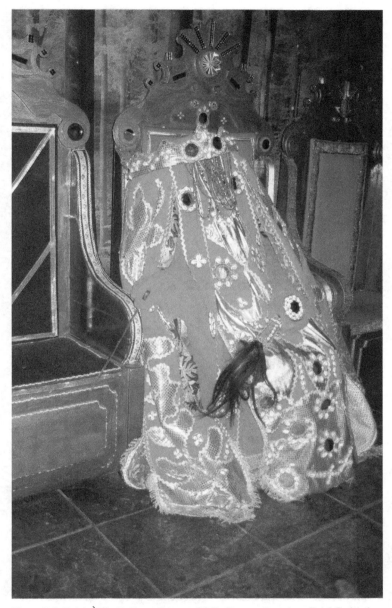

Figure 7.5. Babá Ọ̀lọ́jadé, king of Xango Cá Te Espero, its patron Babá Egúngún.

Figure 7.6. Babá Ọ̀lọ́jadé.

Figure 7.7. Babá Eyéile.

Figure 7.8. Babá Eyéile.

Figure 7.9. Babá Omiloya.

Figure 7.10. Babá Omiloya.

Chapter 8

ORIGINS OF EGÚNGÚN

Bàbáá mi rò gbobi, yóò womo
Bàbá, bó bá mò lé o láyà o yà sinmi.

Father, transmigrate back to earth.
But Father, if it's too tiring, stop and rest.

Yorùbá Egúngún oríkì

This phrase is part of an *oríkì* "praise poem" chanted at a grave
site in Yorùbáland, extolling and coaxing the father to return to
visit once again with the living: "The *oríkì* singer may exhort him
to spring up and make his way quickly over the great distance
that separates the world of the living from that of the dead, but
to stop if it is too tiring."[1]

The practice of Egúngún, as formalized and structured in
Yorùbáland, can be traced back to the Old Ọ̀yọ́ kingdom of
Yorùbá-speaking people ca. sixteenth century.[2] Egúngún,
along with Ọ̀yọ́'s mythic king Ṣàngó and his wife Ọya (mother
of Egúngún), were strongly established there. According to
Babayemi: "The close relationship between Egúngún, Ṣàngó
and Ọya could well be understood if one realizes the fact that
they were all more or less Ọ̀yọ́ institutions."[3] These royal Òrìṣà
maintain a strong bond with Egúngún.[4] We can recognize the
consolidating aspect of Egúngún in Ọ̀yọ́, and its influence on

contemporary Egúngún, and, the importance of Ọya and Ṣàngó vis-à-vis Egúngún both in Africa and in Brazil.

Though historians have placed the origins of Egúngún in Old Ọ̀yọ́, Adedeji proposes that it was adopted from the Nupe in the sixteenth century.[5] It is well beyond the scope of this study to ascertain the originating area of Egúngún before the acknowledged Ọ̀yọ́, especially since the written sources available from that presumed "originating" time period are works of the colonizing Europeans, who observed a culture completely foreign to them and at best wrote naïve descriptions, and at worst considered the populace heathen, primitive, savage, and uneducated. The colonizers had not a clue that what they were observing was far beyond their education and their limited metaphysical and theological training, so it was treated with little importance and zero understanding, described with a hubris as if it did not exist before their arrival. Africans did not just start worshipping their ancestors in the sixteenth century! Egúngún must be understood within a broader frame of both mythic as well as linear time. The structure of rituals may have been codified in Old Ọ̀yọ́, but the veneration of ancestors began long before this. As Robert Smith notes, "Since ancestor worship was apparently practiced by nearly all African societies since early times, it seems likely that the introduction of Egúngún among the Ọ̀yọ́ Yorùbá amounted to an introduction of new rituals and forms rather than of new ideas and beliefs."[6]

The veneration of ancestors and their incorporation into daily life forms an integral part of an indigenous community life in the forest belt of the African continent. Although Egúngún may have been first documented by European observers, they existed long before this. Why should we base the perception of Egúngún—or *any* indigenous African practice—upon the views of an invading colonial enslaving force whose ultimate goal was to Christianize or Islamize the populations and destroy the cultural systems that gave them strength? Fortunately there are other resources, such as the oral history of *oríkìs* (lineage praise poems) and the *ẹsẹ* of Ifá (the countless life-lesson stories comprising the Odù Ifá corpus). These are passed down through the generations through a disciplined apprenticeship system of the oracle priest.

Aremu has argued that "Egúngún tradition is as old as mankind. The lapse in oral tradition and inadequate written records make it very difficult to ascertain the particular time and who first brought or originated the masquerade tradition. Masquerade cult has occupied an important position in the traditional religious beliefs of the Yorùbá people. The Yorùbá are always identified with the ancestral worship."[7]

African and Brazilian practices of Egúngún have ritualistic, structural, and aesthetic differences, but their theory and functions are identical: the recognition that *the dead are not dead*, that they retain an integral role in family and community life, and that the ancestors continue their existence *independent of and not reliant upon those who are left*. Thus the Egúngún are extremely powerful in the spiritual world, to guide and actively participate in the lives of those who venerate them. This independent existence is addressed by Bọlaji Ìdòwú: ". . . the life of the ancestors in the after-life is a reality: it does not depend on the remembrance of them by those who are living on earth. [They] do not for any reason fade into nothing or lapse into any kind of durational retirement."[8]

Multifarious categories of Éguns exist in Yorùbáland: entertainment, witch killers (an antiquated and misleading term), Égun Àgbà (Babá Égun—the eldest), trickster Égun, hunter Égun, and more. Historians and anthropologists have described these types, their functions and, histories.[9] I offer a variety of examples in Africa in the next chapter as part of the comparison with Brazil.

The Egúngún of Brazil seem to be a distillation and amalgam of Egúngún found in specific areas of Yorùbáland, where a large part of the Brazilian slave population originated. The Brazilian Egúngún practice represents not every type or class of Égun that exists in Africa but a particular survival set based on the acknowledgment and veneration of very specific Éguns, such as Babá Olúkòtún, Babá Agboulá, and Babá Bakábaká. These three figures comprise the foremost collective royal ancestors brought from Africa as established on the island of Itaparica.[10] Egúngún is worshipped collectively at the terreiro. In Nigeria, a family might keep an *aṣọ* (Egúngún outfit) for an ancestor in their private shrine; the ritual veneration in Brazil is concentrated in the terreiro in a few select locations: on the island of Itaparica and their offshoots in Rio and Recife.

Several factors contribute to the relatively uncorrupted, uncontaminated, homogenous practice of Egúngún in Brazil, principal among them being its location on the isolated island of Itaparica (*the matrix*, as it were). The tradition was protected through its highly secretive nature; the rigorous vetting of candidates for its membership (you must be chosen by Egúngún);[11] the highly disciplined maintenance of its rituals and philosophy; the physically bounded nature of the terreiros themselves—a separate community bordered by high concrete walls or natural boundaries; the house of Egúngún: the ìgbàlè, the inner chamber housing its deepest secrets; and, unique to Brazil, the barracão itself, a large community meeting space or presentation hall for the Babá Éguns.

These protective factors have enabled Egúngún to thrive in Brazil for over two hundred years. The terreiro represents an entire town—in fact, an entire world—in microcosm. All activities are concentrated within this symbolic setting; all Egúngún live inside the ìgbàlè, safeguarded by the walls of the terreiro. This insulating, protective environment undoubtedly has contributed to the continuity of this tradition. I stress that the perpetuity of the Egúngún cult on Itaparica is a miracle of indomitable commitment, memory, and perseverance.

In Mariano's book, Mãe Estella Azevedo spoke of the terreiro as a world unto itself. Using the terreiro Ilê Axé Opô Afonjá as her model, she emphasized the idea of the terreiro as a microcosm of a complete African town:

> Ilê Axé Opô Afonjá translates as *house of power maintained by Afonjá* (Afonjá is a praise name for Xango). Afonjá is like a small town, a small town that dates back to the times of Mãe Aninha, when she made this place into Africa, placing a house for each *orixá* there. Over there (in Africa) each *orixá* has their own tribe and town, and here she provided a space for each of them, where they have their rites on different days, separately, each according to their own religious precepts.[12]

As noted in my diary, I experienced this sense of the microcosm in my terreiro, not only the physical microcosm, but, in simpler terms: I felt I was transposed to another self-sustaining world, as well as to another time. One's *sense* of time is remolded; the sharp corners of the ticking watch melt away. Mãe Estella claimed that Aninha recreated Africa, and Babá Carlos clearly embraces that same vision. As stated in my diary, at one point during a festival he spread his arms as if to show the world his Ilê, and exalted: "Africa!" Tradition infallibly continues at Xango Cá Te Espero.[13]

"XANGO! CÁ TE ESPERO!"
(XANGO!—HERE I WAIT FOR YOU!)

The name of this terreiro speaks volumes. The simple poetry of this moniker is rich in potential allusion. Cá Te Espero is the name that drew Thompson like a magnet, begging consideration and wonderment. Perhaps this is only my personal tangent; I riff on it, but the poetry remains. The phrase speaks of veneration and enlightenment, the idea of waiting while *making oneself available*. Zen Buddhists say "Wait for the flashing"; that is, enlightenment comes in a flash, in a blink. One must be ready and available.[14]

Figure 8.1. "House of Lord Xangô, here we are waiting for you."

(Doubly apropos as Ṣàngó is the deity of thunder and his cohort, Ọya the mother of Egúngún, is the producer of lightning).

". . . and the Gods; we are here waiting for you."[15]

And there is great humility ascribed to this phrase: "Ṣàngó, I am waiting, resolute in my faith; I am available. We are your sons and daughters carrying on your tradition; we are always here, steadfast in our belief, waiting for you."

In Jacarepaguá the emerging Éguns prod, cajole, strike, tease, dance, admonish, scold, whirl, inspire, astonish, perform, and bless; all movements, actions, and gestures are performed with power and grace. The interplay is athletic and youthful. Thompson states, "Egúngún wants you to surround yourself with youth, they love the vitality of youth."[16]

A celebration, or party for Egúngún is an all-night affair, and the whole festival will last for several days. The drumming is virtuosic, the collective singing tireless; the festival is an imposing communal affair, one that draws members of the terreiro as well as the outside community. The appearance of Babá Égun arrests the collective mind, all those in attendance seem to act and react with a singular consciousness. These joyful events are full of unrelenting energy as visitors from the invisible world are summoned and celebrated, and their blessings petitioned: "A bênção meu pai!" Bless me, my father! The materialization of the spirits in their magnificent cloth assemblages is an inspiring thing to witness.

Chapter 9

CHANGE AND CONTINUITY
From Africa to Brazil

Egúngún in Brazil is a reflection and continuation of the Egúngún of Yorùbáland in West Africa. The most striking example of clear continuity is the physical form and aesthetic of the Egúngún dress—the *aṣọ*, the clothing of Egúngún—as shown by the pictures herein. Henry Drewal states: "While the materials that constitute the various ensembles [in Brazil] may be different from those used in Africa, the *aṣọ*, that completely envelops the dancing spirit, is structured much like those of àgbà (elder) Egúngún of Nigeria and the Republic of Benin."[1] The stunning aesthetic of dress is equally ornate on both continents, equally spectacular, equally riveting in its arresting visual qualities.

Also corresponding is the manner in which Egúngún communicates, the timbre ranging from the well-documented gravelly utterance—likened to the colobus monkey[2]—to a high-pitched, flute-like sound found on both sides of the Atlantic.[3] When I asked Babá Carlos about these two sounds and the voice of Egúngún, his reply was charged with meaning: "It is not right to say that Egúngún has a voice. Égun doesn't emanate a voice. The sound that Egúngún emanates is called *eegi*, it is a sound from beyond the grave, produced by the wind blowing through the trees, specifically the bamboo grove known as *dancô*. Between those two nuances lie an infinite spectrum of *eegi* sounds.[4] Like the wind itself, its timbre is of infinite range."

As in Africa, Brazil maintains the exclusively male makeup of the Egúngún brotherhood, with limited but specific roles and titles for women.[5] The male exclusivity of Egúngún is balanced by the Gèlèdè society, dedicated to the archetypal power of women, the Ìyàmi. To my knowledge, the Gèlèdè society survives less vigorously in Brazil than in Yorùbáland.[6]

The role of the attendants of Egúngún is also similar to that in Africa: the atókùn (or amúìşan) in Yorùbáland, and the Amux-ian in Brazil utilize the àtòrì whips known as ìşan (ìxan [P]) to separate the spectators from the Egúngún, the living from the dead.[7] They use the ìşan to guide and control the Egúngún.[8] The Òjè also wield the ìşan, striking the floor three times to summon Egúngún.[9] Rules of behavior for the spectators are similar, too; it is a common admonition not to touch Egúngún in any way.[10] Egúngún's ability to perform seemingly impossible movements and acrobatics is also comparable—likewise the boundless energy they possess and manifest.

More important than the outward similarities manifested is the societies' raison d'être: to invoke and return to earth the ancestors, the ará òrun—visitors from heaven, people from beyond—to corporealize within the fantastically decorated cloak-like garments known as aşo,[11] to bestow blessings, cleanse the community of evil, grant petitions (e.g., children to the barren), and maintain and insure social equilibrium. Equally alike is the conception of who the ancestors are. According to Ìdòwú, the Yorùbá possess the "invincible conviction that those who departed from this world have only exchanged this life for another. Primarily 'Ancestor Worship' is an *extension into infinity* [italics mine] of the family activities of the earth."[12] I believe this philosophical sentiment to be wholly in line with that of Brazilian Egúngún adherents.

Another important similarity is in the African and Brazilian reactions of the living when in the presence of Egúngún. There is an aura of electric excitement; the palpable delight, love, and affection humans have for their manifested ancestors is a joyous

thing to behold. It is mirrored in the sheer boundless energy and
enthusiasm on the part of the Egúngún themselves.

A VISIT TO AFRICA

In the spring of 2019 I visited Nigeria to attend a five-day Ifá
festival. It took place at my temple in Ibadan, Ilé Okànràn Onílẹ̀,
hosted by my spiritual brother, friend, and mentor, Babá Adewale
Bógunmbẹ̀, the àwíṣẹ of Idoland. One of the nights was dedicated to bringing out Egúngún. Around 6 p.m. Egúngún seemed
to appear suddenly and soon the patio was bristling with action
and virtuosic drumming. Babá explained something to me: "Any
place prepared for Egúngún to come out is called ìgbàlẹ and
can be anywhere according to the wish of the Egúngún priest."
Ìgbàlẹ is also the same name of the secreted room in the Brazilian terreiro where Egúngún is invoked. Egúngún arrived and
danced and moved with unstoppable exuberance. The patio and
entrance hummed with invisible vitality as the entrance to the
compound was now filled with different Egúngún; the electric
energy reminded me so much of Brazil.

From this point at the entrance to Babá's compound, Egúngún
seemed to fly as they took off down the dirt road, the *abala*
panels fanning out like whirlwinds, the glorious colors high-
lighted against the beautiful African twilight. The energy of
the Egúngún was just like I experienced in Brazil—wild and
unbridled—movement like quicksilver, turning on a dime from
a sedentary position to bolt down the road, impossibly fast over
the rutted hard-dirt surface, stopping to spin his colorful lappets,
manifesting his mother Ọya's signature whirlwind.

At times cars or motorcycles would do their best to get by,
at other times trucks—perhaps loaded down with countless
bottles of potable water—had to wait until the Egúngún moved
or was coaxed into moving by the atọ́kùn. They paraded down

Figure 9.1. Egúngún coming out of *ìgbàle* during annual Ifa/Òrìṣà festivals of Babá Adewale Bógunmbẹ̀, the Awise of Idoland, Ibadan, Nigeria.

the road far into the neighboring area, the drummers following and the atọ̀kùn keeping up and guiding them and the crowd. The difference in Brazil is that Egúngún activity is compact and localized within the terreiro, a closed-area compound, a walled-off microcosm of a town onto itself.

At other times the atọ̀kùn would act out a dramatic fight with the *ìṣan* as they ran down the road accompanying the Egúngún, a fierce exhibition. When I asked Adewale about this, he responded: "It is a reenactment of the struggles our ancestors had to go through, so we do not forget how much they struggled and sacrificed." I observed similar (though more playful) activity in Brazil. Brazilian Egúngún worship and ritual is very organized and disciplined, its activities restricted to the terreiro. Egúngún in Yorùbáland roam free not only within the compound but also out in the dirt roads of the neighboring area, blessing the community and everyone in it.

Perhaps the most important parallel I experienced in Africa was the feeling of deep respect, love, and gratitude between the living and those who have passed on to another life; it was as deeply felt there as I had ever experienced in my terreiro in

Brazil. The adoration and reverence of Egúngún, and the reason for their existence, is unmistakably equivalent.

At one point an Egúngún came up to me and embraced me, communicating in his gravelly *eegi*; it was a great blessing for me. This would have been very unusual in Brazil; Egúngún does not embrace people there, though sometimes the Egúngún touch you with flowers or a sword that's part of their aṣọ. I did not telegraph my surprise, and I was very moved by the moment. The Amuxian in Brazil keep the Egúngún separated from the living with their ìxan, and we are forbidden to touch them. It is the same in Africa, and as Adewale explained: "Babá, that doesn't happen to everyone. They can touch you; you cannot touch them. They might embrace you to take away pain." This was very poignant for me.

I cannot comment on initiatory or ritual continuity; I know nothing about the initiation process in Yorùbáland, nor could I speak about it if I did. This is a hidden body of knowledge; it is viewed as one of the *awos* (mysteries) that came from heaven, only revealed to the initiate.[13]

Festivals for Egúngún in Brazil are accompanied by continuous singing and drumming, and there is an extensive liturgy of songs, in Portuguese or in a combination of Portuguese and Yorùbá languages. The presence of the Yorùbá language in the Brazilian liturgy is another example of African continuity. There is a rare LP of Egúngún songs recorded during a festival at Ilê Agboulá in Bahia.[14] I could not determine whether the melody and rhythmic structures of these songs are equivalent to any song from Yorùbáland, but the use of Yorùbá is clear in the song titles. For instance, *Agboulá Ago Onílè* (Agboulá, asking for permission to enter); this song, according to the notes on the LP, refers to Babá Agboulá: "When he is on the earth everything is filled with joy." Another example is *Egúngún Kigbalé* (Egúngún greets ìgbàlẹ): "Through this song, the ancestors are called to show themselves, materializing in the world of the living."[15] These two brief examples suggest a rich area for further study.

WHAT IS THE DIFFERENCE BETWEEN
EGÚNGÚN SOCIETIES IN BRAZIL AND AFRICA?

Though we can see the obvious similarities of dress, movement, communication, and spiritual and social function, Egúngún obviously did not arrive on the shores of Bahia fully formed. Henry Drewal posits: "The first thing the arriving slaves would have done is to give thanks to their ancestors and appeal for their survival in a land that they didn't want and didn't expect, and to honor them in some way. *They arrived empty-handed, not empty-headed.*"[16] Indeed, the recreation of the Egúngún cult was and is nothing short of a miracle. Liberated Africans and their families kept this tradition alive within a tight-knit community; it thrived singularly on the island of Itaparica and eventually branched out from that matrix. How Egúngún was worshipped and the aesthetic of the dress would be based on what those arriving African priests knew from their homeland; this was bolstered by trips back and forth to Africa, the so-called "second migration." (I explore these ideas in chapter 12.) From this starting point Brazilian Egúngún was reconstituted and continues to thrive and evolve, while retaining a strong foundational link to Africa.

Perhaps the most obvious difference between the societies of Brazil and Africa is that Egúngún in Brazil is localized. There are only three active and acknowledged centers of Egúngún: Bahia (on the Isle of Itaparica), Rio de Janeiro, and Recife. (Starting in Itaparica, it branched out first to Rio, then Recife.)[17] The members of these centers work together and acknowledge and support each other, traveling to each other's terreiros to work and participate in ceremonies and annual festivals. For example, for my Amuxian initiation ceremony, Ojés from Ilê Obaerin (House of Obaerin) in Pernambuco, Recife, and Ilê Agboulá in Itaparica traveled to participate. Members of my terreiro reciprocate at their initiations and festivals; for example, Babá Carlos travels frequently because of his elder rank. This yields a familial closeness within all three major centers; it also establishes multiple witnesses to ceremonies, an all-important validation for an individual member.

Precise records are kept of initiations; this level of validation is crucial to the inviolability of the cult and insures that the secrecy and masonic-like brotherhood is maintained. There are admonishments that one might see on Facebook; an elder of the society will rebuke a particular person for claiming membership in the cult and state that no record of this person's initiation exists.[18] It is a very closed and punctiliously documented society.

If I travel to any of these terreiros I am accepted as a brother. When I arrived at Ilê Agboulá (as I describe in Chapter 6), I was simply asked my level of initiation, since, in my case, they already knew who I was. We spoke familiarly of Babá Carlos and his son Carlos Jr.'s recent initiation that took place there.

Another significant difference is that, in Africa, babaláwos can perform some Egúngún functions. Babá Adewale informed me that: "Babaláwos can complete certain things, but there are separate Egúngún priests, and initiation into the Egúngún society is a separate bundle of activities."[19] This is very different in Brazil, where babaláwos essentially have had no active role in Candomblé or Egúngún since the last Brazilian babaláwo, Martiniano Eliseu do Bonfim, passed away in the 1940s.[20] The full responsibility for Egúngún is with the members of the society.[21]

As far as categorizing Egúngún, there are two basic types of Egúngún in Brazil: the aparaká and the Babá Égun (elder Égun—Égun Àgbà).[22] The aparaká is an undeveloped spirit, a phase that all potential Egúngún must pass through.[23] A more heterogenous categorization of Babá Égun exists in Yorùbáland, as the broad categories and individual design differ from town to town, and region to region.

Although in Brazil we do not see the myriad classes of Egúngún that exist in Yorùbáland, they are still diverse within a smaller sphere. The Egúngún in Brazil can be entertaining but they are not mere entertainers; they are acrobatic but not acrobats; they will jest but are not jesters. They are all Babá Égun or aparaká, and all Éguns are treated with great deference. Within these two categories there is great variety of Babá Égun, less so of aparaká because of the simpler nature of aparaká's design. The decorative style and diverse aesthetic of Babá Égun is broad, reflecting the variety of those persons of great character who might become Egúngún. Nevertheless, in Brazil a more homogenous manifestation of Egúngún appears than in Africa, maintaining direct common roots from the matrix of Ilha Itaparica. (I explore the aparaká further in chapter 10.)

Three elder Egúngún, which Babá Carlos likened to a "holy trinity," include Babá Olúkọ̀tún (King of the kings, Lord on the right side of Olódùmarè), Babá Bakabaká (representing Babaluaiye), and Babá Agboulá (representing Xangô), all originating from the island of Itaparica. It is the terrerieo of Ilê Agboulá on Itaparica that is considered the matrix for all of Egúngún in Brazil.[24]

There is a consistency to the magnificently decorated aesthetic of the aṣọ in Brazil. Additionally, there is the similar construction for Egúngún outfits, the shape of the costume with the long assemblage flowing from a flat top to the floor—completely enveloping the materialized spirit—with abala lappets that fan out while spinning or moving back and forth to deliver aṣe to the adherents. There are some variations: there is an Egúngún with a large square top that can change his height from very small to stretch out almost to the ceiling—when I was transfixed by the appearance of this Egúngún, Fabio touched my arm and said: "Don't stare too much at that one!"[25] There is an Egúngún with an elaborate headdress of an indigenous Indian representing the Caboclo of Brazil, and as previously mentioned, I witnessed a small Egúngún with a very simple, unadorned outfit, Babá Àlejò, "a visitor." Thus, variation appears within the assemblage design of the Égun Àgbà, or elder Egúngún. Although a basic shape

Figure 9.2. Babá Àlejò, "the visitor," getting doused with perfume by elder *mae de santo*, Ogum Bonam.

remains, there are some additional constructs as mentioned above. One unique aspect of Brazilian Egúngún is the splashing of perfume on the Babá Éguns, typically done by the women. Babá Carlos explained that this was done to make the Éguns feel at home as much as possible—the scent used is that of plants and its fragrance is reminiscent of the forest grove.

Where Brazilian Egúngún assemblage might be considered more homogenous in the basic shape, African Egúngún is very diverse in its multiplicity of manifestations. There are numerous types—sometimes employing the same generic name for different types of Egúngún in different townships or areas—and potentially endless names of individual family Egúngún. Nor, historically, has every town in Yorùbáland had Egúngún, or have it currently. Each town or area that venerates Egúngún will have its own particular type of Egúngún and history, and its own aesthetic of aṣọ construction particular to that area. And Egúngún in Yorùbáland includes not only Nigeria, as Dana Rush relates: "this strong tradition currently proliferates throughout southwestern Nigeria, southern Bénin and Togo, and into Ghana."[26]

The categories of Egúngún vary from town to town.[27] In an interview in which I asked Babá Adewale about these, he listed the following: (1) *Eyo* for Lagos; (2) *Igunu-ko*—the "super-tall Égun"; (3) *Layewu,* the hunters Égun; and (4) *Paaka Ilesanyin,* which relates to òrun/Ifá.[28] My examination of two additional sources revealed further variations and classifications.

Houlberg points to three generic types found in Ikenne, a Remo Yorùbá town: (1) *Alubata* (the one who plays the drum), the body of the costume made of strips of narrow-band cloth; (2) *Idomole,* having elaborate, colorful, patchwork panels; and (3) *Onidan,* the owner of miracles. (Houlberg's article also offers excellent detailed descriptions.)[29]

Thompson lists five generic types: (1) *Agan,* senior Egúngún; (2) *Bàbá Parikoko,* with long flowing robes "trailing fifty yards behind him"; (3) *Onidan,* miracle workers; (4) *Alabala,* displayers-of-cloth; and (5) *Olokiti,* tumblers.[30] Commenting on this great diversity, Wolff states: "In any particular locality, *Egúngún* masquerades come in many forms or generic types, which are emically labeled."[31] This briefest glimpse into the vast reservoir of varietal richness found in African Egúngún gives some idea of the complexity of Egúngún in Yorùbáland. Contrast this, based on my observations as a member of the society, to the more homogenous manifestation in Brazil, which retains diversity within fewer generic categories.[32] This difference reveals yet another area of study open to further investigation.

HOW OLD IS EGÚNGÚN IN BRAZIL AND AFRICA?

Egúngún has existed in Brazil since the early 1800s, while the age of Egúngún in Africa—and the ultimate age of Brazilian Egúngún—is unknowable. Modern scholars list dates of relatively recent origin, but these are in no way reliable. As noted, they may point to a codification of a particular Egúngún society, but as understood through Ifá verses and oral *oríkì* (memorized stories of the Ifá divination corpus and praise poems, respectively), Egúngún is as old as humanity and must be understood in that way, i.e., in mythological time.[33] George Brandon eloquently states: "As manifestations of the communal ancestors, the Egúngún maskers embody a force still resounding from the time when all human institutions first came into existence."[34]

European colonists and missionaries were the first to write about the Yorùbá traditional societies. Since Yorùbá history is an oral history, the search for written documents of antiquity is fruitless. The true source is within the staggeringly large memories of the Ifá priests and the griots, and in the mythology of the Òrìṣà.[35]

In the Ifá corpus the Odù Ogbè Ọ̀ṣá (Ogbèríkúsá) tells one of these stories about the origin of Egúngún, sent from heaven to make the world stable. From Babayemi:

> [T]he Egúngún were heavenly spirits. After the creation of the world, the earth was not stable. All the Òrìṣà tried their best but they were not successful until Olódùmarè sent down the *ébórá* (heavenly spirits) from heaven. Where these *ébórá* landed was Ìgbo Ìgbàle (sacred grove). They had to disguise themselves [using the costumed dress] to carry necessary rituals to the four corners of the earth; after that the world became stable. These *ébórá* were therefore called *se aiyé gún*, "those who make the earth stable." And it was from this that Egúngún originated. This Odù explains the political and social foundations of Egúngún in society. The Egúngún rids society of all forces of instability.[36]

Though the contemporary manifestation of Egúngún in Brazil and Yorùbáland reveals some differences, the basic aspects and

concepts are very much alike. Nevertheless, including metempirical evidence such as the story above (along with many others)
leads us to a greater and truer understanding of Egúngún as it
exists in both Brazil and Yorùbáland.

Chapter 10

A MYSTERIOUS WIND

Aparaká

A square of fabric on a horizontal stick dancing, wavering, shooting forth, lunging, shakily quivering side to side, the simplicity of their cloth medium a visual clue of their lesser status: they accompany the elder Éguns, who are draped in magnificent cloth finery and symbolic decoration. These are the aparaká, the intermediate stage of an ancestor on its journey to consecration as a Babá Égun. Babá Carlos describes the aparaká thus: "They are the protectors of Babá Égun. Like Exú is the protector of the Òrìṣà, the aparaká are the protectors of Egúngún. Aparaká is the transitional stage the spirit must traverse before becoming immortalized as Egúngún."[1]

Witnessing the aparaká in my initial encounter with Egúngún at Xango Cá Te Espero was an experience of bewilderment and surprise. I was not alone in my wonderment, as this sentiment was echoed by my guides for the evening, Ailton Benedito de Sousa and his daughter Luciana, a daughter of Oya. As the only two persons who spoke English, they rescued me from my frustrating incomprehension at not being able to communicate. I remember Ailton saying: "Yes, the Egúngún are astonishing. But it is the aparaká that really amaze me: *for they are like a mysterious wind.*"

Thompson related the following: "They are scary because they are so abstract."[2] I felt the same way. The abstraction magnifies their otherworldliness. Where the spectacle of Egúngún is breathtaking, confounding, and deeply mysterious, they at least have a vague semblance of human physicality in terms of a recognizable shape. But the abstract aparaká and their powerful movements are truly intimidating and frightening to viewers, to the point of sending folks behind the locked door of a kitchen, or whatever room available, should they get caught outside the barracão at the same time.

The aparaká are defined as spirits in a transitional state that embody a primal spiritual force; they are not yet settled, do not fully grasp their own identity as spirits, and have not gone through the years of spiritual tempering necessary to become Babá Égun. The simplicity of their cloth rendering indicates their lower standing. They do not speak. They are the embodiment of a formal provisional state for a spirit; only those who were Ojé in life need not go through the phase of aparaká. (I outline these transitional stages of afterlife more fully in my interview with Babá Carlos.)

A North American writer succinctly described an aparaká:

Before long an *aparaká* made it to the entrance, and peered around it at the audience. All I could see was a white cross on a sheet of dark blue fabric. The *aparaká* retreated, and then came back and entered the *barracão*. The costume of the *aparaká* consists of two large square sheets of cloth sewn together on three sides. The result is a virtually two-dimensional square surface—a flat plane that twists and contorts as it lunges about the room.[3]

In Nigeria, precursors of the Brazilian Égun aparaká have been described. While reporting significant variations of Egúngún throughout Yorùbáland, along with some intriguing similarities, Schlitz observed, "the Egúngún type called *paka* (*paaraka*) in Iganna has swirling panels of cloth suspended from a horizontal stick.[4] And Pemberton describes them as lineage ancestors; they could be a variety of shapes.[5] And Drewal relates: "In Ilaro there are no *paka*, and the term is recalled only as an ancient name for all Egúngún."[6]

Wande Abímbólá referred to the aparaká as *pààká*: "the name of a small Egúngún owned by young men."[7] These are all clues to the origins of the physical appearance of aparaká in Brazil. The closest physical resemblance is the above-mentioned reference to the horizontal stick and cloth from the Western Ọ̀yọ́ Egúngún tradition in Iganna. Thompson succinctly describes the aparaká as "walking rectangles, in pure white, green, or blue and black cotton without embellishment"; they are "*distant relatives*" (italics mine) of the above-mentioned predecessors.[8]

THEY ARE HERE BUT THEY ARE NOT HERE

With the following quote, Karin Barber references an *oriki* chanter calling Ṣàngó down from his place: ". . . 'lágbede méjì ayé òun ọ̀run,' '*halfway between heaven and earth . . . ,*'"[9] the in-between meeting point of *aiê*—the material world and the human societies created upon it—and ọ̀run, the invisible habitat of Egúngún and Òrìṣà.

Egúngún represent an in-between world. For example, when we called the spirit of my godmother in Brazil, we had to wait till earthly in-between time—the twilight dusk between afternoon and evening—to reach into the spirit world. And performing the obrigação brought us into a liminal state: in between the physical and spiritual realms. Between these two worlds of the living and the dead, the Amuxian serves as a buffer, wielding his ixan to keep the Egúngún at an appropriate distance from those present, when Egúngún visits aiê. To touch the dress of the Egúngún is forbidden and dangerous. Only the mystically charged ixan can touch the clothes of Egúngún.[10]

Egúngún are permeated with this aura of in-between-ness, of being here but not being here. They are a mystery wrapped up in impenetrable cloth in an abstract, more-or-less human shape. Not human but not not-human. A nonhuman shape in an Egúngún represents a collective entity or abstract idea, according to Dos Santos: "some aspect related to death."[11]

Egúngún is an ineffable presence, yet at the same time a physical reality, a dream colliding with waking life, an immeasurable immensity. Egúngún harbors unfathomable mysteries and limitless potentiality represented by these materialized masters of an unseen world, ritually dressed phantoms.[12] Babátunde Lawal eloquently states: "The voluminous costume of the Egúngún conceals the unknowable and yet reveals humans' infinite potential for spiritual transformation."[13]

They echo the enigma of the caul in the unborn: in Yorùbáland, a child born with a caul over the face is automatically a member of the Egúngún cult, receiving the name of *ato*, one of the mythical, ancient names of Egúngún triplets.[14] (Abímbọ́lá additionally ascribes the name *ato* and subsequent Egúngún membership to a female born holding the umbilical cord.)[15] Thompson describes it thusly: in Africa, "when a person is born with a caul over their eyes, their face is covered. And one of the aspects of Egúngún is facelessness. Égun doesn't have a face. He is just movement and breath. The caul, the facelessness—they are here, they are gone, but they are here."[16]

Thompson continues: "How powerful that is. If your son's born with a caul over his face, even non-Yorùbá, it's a form of in-utero masking."[17] And, relating the dead to the unborn, facelessness as a state of transition to and from the netherworlds: "Facelessness of the dead-returning mirrors the facelessness of the infant arriving."[18]

BETWEEN TWO WORLDS: CLOTH AS CURRENCY

In West African and Brazilian Egúngún tradition, cloth is used as a protective and commemorative barrier between the living and the dead. Cloth separates the two worlds while indicating their border. Universally, cloth seems to function within an instinctual human response to covering the dead. When a dead body lies in the street, medical workers pull a sheet over his or her face, "out of respect"; it's so instinctive—acknowledging and physically creating this boundary between life and death—that this person has joined the ranks of the "faceless ones." There is great love, tenderness, and reverence in these actions. There is something deeply sacred about death. When a corpse is enshrouded in a body bag, we reference Egúngún (however abstractly): it is covered from head to toe; details of the human form are no longer evident; the shapelessness of the body bag mythically transforms the corpse into Egúngún. People always intuit the appropriateness of covering the dead. When Trayvon Martin (1995–2012) was so brutally murdered in the United States, the person who discovered him reflexively covered his body and face with his own jacket—a touching moment of instinctual humanity.

Mummies from ancient Egypt were shrouded. Around the world, humans cover the dead to separate the worlds, while commemorating and honoring the transition. When the dead are covered in this simple respectful gesture, they are converted to the shapelessness of Egúngún in the West African tradition.

Thompson articulates the idea of *cloth as currency*, as a way to honor the dead:

> The proper way of honoring the ancestors among the Yorùbá, the Congo and others, is to bring them gifts of cloths. The currency (the medium), the appropriate gift is cloth. When we bring back that ancestral spirit known as *nyombo* in Congo, what he wants is lots of red railroad blankets, that are then turned into a mummy. The mummies become desiccated; so you can have one, two, three, or four ancestors inside a single encapsulating garment.

He continues, "But also the Yorùbá. What is Egúngún but many honorific givings of ritual loyalty to the cause (of *iwa rere*, good character and upright living) and giving cloth to the ancestors. These rituals are practiced across broad parts of the forest belt of Africa": "In the Eja funerals of the Niger delta, the dead are laid out in a pile of cloth until it disappears, as if the deceased were nothing but cloth itself. Over and over again, cloth is the proper medium for letting the ancestors know that they are loved."[19]

WILL YOU BUY ME A NEW SET OF CLOTHES?

The cloth of Egúngún—the *aṣọ* [Y] *axo* [P],—the all-important aspect of Egúngún, forms the temporary house that Babá Égun will reside in during his earthly visit (also known as the *opá* in Brazil). The word most commonly used for Egúngún's clothes and generically for Egúngún themselves, is *masquerade*. That word is inaccurate; it is the term of the colonizer. The word suggests something hidden—something false, a pretense—when in fact, Egúngún outfits reveal or reflect the spirit's highest potentiality and all that was good in a person when they were alive.

Early Europeans in Africa who witnessed Egúngún described them as "masquerades," their reference being the masked balls of European elites; missionaries also used the term deprecatingly as a synonym for "humbug," referencing the natives' presumed gullibility.[20] When I asked Henry Drewal his opinion of the term, he responded: "I don't like it. There is no easy translation for it. I like what Abidoun calls 'power concealed,' that relates to the indigenous meaning of the word."[21] And, according to Adedeji: "Before the usage of the word *Egúngún* gained currency, the Yorùbá word for 'masquerade' was simply Babá (father), or *ẹbọrá* (spirit)."[22] It is *not* accepted as a correct or useable term in Brazil. According to Omari: "The head and other officials of the Egúngún society, Seu Domingo, Babá Carlos Ojé Dúdú, and others, repeatedly emphasized to me the inappropriateness of the term 'masquerade' to describe the aṣọ Égun. They are *not masquerades*."[23]

In Yorùbáland, the clothing for Egúngún was that familiar to the Égun being invoked during his lifetime, his own clothes even, facilitating the appearance of that spirit even as a concluding visit before the spirit took its final leave. This function developed into the costumes or dress of Babá Éguns, whereby that elevated personage's dress would represent a refined rendering of the person's highest qualities. Ìdòwú states: "The body is wrapped in all the clothes which are meant for the deceased person's use in the next life."[24] Thompson reflects on the symbolism of a magnificently ornate Egúngún costume as embodying all that is good in a person: "The mask (costume) stands revealed, not as an image of a man as he lived on earth, but as the redistilled shaping of his finest powers."[25] And Aremu rightly considers the clothes of Egúngún as commemorative: "Egúngún worshippers see the various costumes as commemorative clothes."[26] His teacher Ṣàngódare Alimi of Taraa in Ogbomoso states: "We have got to honor our deities and ancestors with their preferential colored clothes in order to secure favors. These clothes stand as the *magnetic forces that draw us near to them*" [italics mine].[27]

In both Brazil and Africa, the clothes of Egúngún reveal and reflect the nature of the being summoned. Brazilian professor of architecture at UFBA Fábio Macêdo Velame considers the sacred *opá* (*aṣọ*) "an architecture of moving cloths." He writes: "The sacred *opá* is a shelter of the spirits of the illustrious dead of the community, a temporary residence of the ancestors, a house made of cloths for the dead woven by their descendants, a house without doors, windows, walls or roofs, a house where only the dead have a right to live."[28]

Egúngún are understood as the spirit entering the multilayered cloth assemblages—his clothes—which form a house for the spirit. The mystical, spiritual element of the clothing cannot be overstated: the aṣọ—the dress or cloth assemblage—represents the Égun according to his background: an Égun who was a priest of Ṣàngó in his life would be adorned with brilliant red shining cloth with the sawtooth panels of Nupe influence,[29] replete with embroidered appliqué of lightning bolts and the *Ose Ṣàngó*, the ubiquitous double-headed axe symbol of multidirectional power. But as the particular dress of a Babá Égun is beyond mere aesthetic representation, its deeper symbolic levels must be considered. Writing about Abeokuta in Yorùbáland, Wolff reports: "The fabric also plays an important ritual role, taking on a supernatural aura with use in costumes, the cloth is a way of tying the Egúngún spirit, also known as *ará ọrun* (citizen of heaven), to the cultural world of the living by enclosing it in a man-made cage of fabric."[30]

In Yorùbáland, "Only when all parts of the ensemble are brought together and joined in a ritual act does the spirit of the Egúngún enter the costume. The costume itself . . . acts as a shrine for the Egúngún spirit."[31] In Brazil the outfits are sewn only by the Ọjẹs. These assemblages require considerable time and money; the enormous skill and training needed is passed down through apprenticeship.[32]

When I first visited Xango Cá Te Espero in 2005, Bàbá Ọlójadé asked me: "Will you buy me a new set of clothes?" The simplicity of this statement made it clear the way in which the Egúngún themselves thought of their cloth assemblages—not *masquerade* or *costume*—but simply as the clothes they wear.

Chapter 11

MOTHER OF NINE

*Ọya ni yi ti o d'Òrìṣà Odòna se aiye
o dòna se ọrun.*

She guards the road into the world and
guards the road to heaven.[1]

ỌYA

Ọya is the mother of Egúngún and Òrìṣà of the wind. She occupies
a special status in the world of the dead. Mariano states: "When
we praise the mistress of winds and storms, we also remember
that she is the conductor of souls, and the mother of all *Éguns*."[2]
She is the owner of the cemetery, associated with the buffalo and
the whirlwind, an important wife of Ṣàngó, and the bearer of nine
children, "*anomalous beings*," the last of them being Egúngún:
"*the ancestor who returns*." Gleason identified her manifestation
through riparian physicality as the Niger River, which splits into
multiple estuaries as it empties into the sea.[3] She is the whirlwind
tearing the tops off of trees, the bringer of unexpected changes,
a warrior woman who accompanies Xango in battles.

Ọya also claims special status in the marketplace. Gleason
states: "To the leader of the market women in Yorùbá com-

munities she offers special protection and encouragement in negotiation with civil authorities and arbitration of disputes among peers. Thus, one may speak of Ọya as patron of feminine leadership, of intelligent persuasive charm."[4]

Ọya claims the highest status and respect in Brazil and throughout the Americas; her children are regarded with special awe. As mother of Egúngún, she is fundamental to Candomblé/Egúngún orthodoxy; she is also central to many of the creation myths concerning the birth of Egúngún. Gleason emphasizes this relationship: "In Nigeria she has given birth to an extraordinary clan of *ancestral apparitions* [italics mine] clothed in bulky, billowing cloth who perform at festivals for the dead."[5]

One of her appellations in Brazil and Cuba is *Yansan*, meaning "mother-of-nine" in Yorùbá: *Ìyá*, mother; *mesan*, nine. According to certain Egúngún creation myths, Ọya had nine sons; the first eight were born mute. The ninth could speak, but only in the guttural voice of the *ìjìmèrè* (*pataguenon*) monkey: this *anomalous* ninth son was Egúngún.[6] Several myths portray the birth of Egúngún and Ọya and her nine children, Thompson offers this version:

> Ọya is supposed to have had difficulty in bearing children. According to Ifá as recited in Nigeria, her nine ancestral spirit-children were produced with the help of termite-mound magic.[7] Soldier ants defaced Egúngún, the youngest of those "born in the anthill"; so he had to go about veiled. . . . There is a matching myth from Brazil: Shango takes Ọya sexually. The first eight children are born mute. The ninth, because Ọya has properly sacrificed, does speak, but with the strange, gravelly voice some associate with the ìjìmèrè monkey.[8]

Ọya claims special status of being able to traverse both heavenly and earthly realms—moving freely between the nine spheres of ọrun, the celestial dwelling place of the divinities, the Òrìṣà,

and the Éguns, the souls of the dead. Robert Voeks describes
ọrun as a series of nine energy levels of concentric rings: "The
Òrìṣà Iansã is said to have special migratory powers, as she is
the only spiritual entity capable of moving freely among the
nine spaces."[9]

Thompson echoed this idea in a discussion of the Nupe, the
Ndkogboya—the equivalency of Egúngún in Nupe—and the
spectacular Ọya assemblage that shoots straight up into the air
and back down again: "I'm sure you've seen Ọya going up and
down. But of course, that has a meaning. *That means her access
is wider than ours* [italics mine]. And one means of the access is
the tomb, the cemetery portion of her power. The other end of
access is the purest blinding light in heaven."[10]

This migratory power forces us to think of Ọya in more complex terms; she resides in the cemetery to receive the souls of
the dead, and yet can traverse the highest realms of heaven,
while her influence in earthly matters is in the wind itself, in the
marketplace, as cohort of Ògún and Ṣàngó, and as a ruler in her
own right. According to Wande Abímbọ́lá:

> Ọya was a potentate in her own right, not just a queen in the
> sense of being a wife of Ṣàngó. She was a ruler of Irá. She is one
> of the most important images of womanhood. Here was a woman
> who was much more powerful than her husband. She was still
> married to the husband, she has children, she was a mother, she
> was a potentate, and she was the most powerful Òrìṣà of all.

The following song alludes to this:

> *Ọya dolú*
> *Ègàn ò royin*
> *Ọya dolú*
> *Ègàn ò royin*
> *Ègàn ò mọ̀ le wí pé kóyin má ṣe dùn o.*

Ọya dolú
Ègàn ò royin

Ọya has become a potentate,
Derision does not affect honey.
Ọya has become a potentate,
Derision does not affect honey,
Derision cannot prevent honey from being sweet,
Ọya has become a potentate,
Derision does not affect honey.[11]

Nine paths of Ọya are widely acknowledged in Brazil: *Ọya Bale* (shortened from ìgbàlẹ, the sacred room in which Egúngún resides) is the commonly accepted path of Ọya as mother of Egúngún.[12] But the relationship between Egúngún and Ọya is much richer and more complex, according to Babá Carlos. When speaking with me on this subject, he revealed that within the nine paths of Ọya are actually five qualities or aspects specifically associated with Ọya's relationship with Egúngún, and that the path of Ọya that gave birth to Egúngún is *Ọya Onirá*. He elaborated on the different paths of Ọya relating to Egúngún during my first interview:

There are nine qualities to Ọya, and five that deal specifically with Égun [É*gum* (P)].

[1.] *Ọya Onirá*, she is the one who gave birth to Egúngún. Ọya of Onirá, *a senhora de Ira*—The Lady of Ira. (The city of Ira is the abode of Ọya—it was in Ira that she mythically disappeared into the ground when she had grown tired of living on the earth.)[13] So Ọya Onirá is the mother of Égum.

[2.] *Ọya Bale* is in charge of the guardianship of Égum, protecting Égum because he was under the earth, under the stones, always hiding, keeping out of sight. The temple where Égum lives and is guarded is *Lesayin, Lesayin Ìgbàlẹ*. Ọya Bale is in charge of the guardianship of the Lesayin.

[3.] *Oya Pada* is the hunter of Égum, hunter for identification, spirit hunter looks for people.

[4.] *Oya Egum Onitá*, who is the only one who can come out next to the Babá Égums. She can lead ahead of them, in front of the Égums when they come out. She is the only one with the power to lead them, because she has the power of conducting. Not even mother Onirá herself or Oya Padá can lead Égum. Oya Égum Onitá is the *siwayu* (leader/head) of *bogbo* (all) Égum; she goes ahead of all Égums. It is as if she is the conductor, or *bateador*, like in the *escolas de samba* during carnival.

[5.] *Oya Bagan*. She lives inside the cemetery; we cannot be burnt or cremated, we have to be buried in a shallow grave because when we are buried in a shallow grave we are being restored to Oya Bagan's womb.[14]

To summarize the five Oyas who govern all things to do with Egúngún:

1. Oya Onirá—*a senhora de Irá*, mother of Egúngún.
2. Oya Bale—the guardian of Egúngún (*'Bale* shortened from ìgbàle, the sacred Egúngún grove).
3. Oya Padá—the hunter, identifier.
4. Oya Onitá—leader of all the Éguns, "like the conductor of a carnival group."
5. Oya Bagan—who resides in the cemetery, the womb to which we are restored.

Through my training as an initiate of Egúngún in Brazil, I learned that the information concerning Oya and Egúngún is much deeper than previously known or commonly acknowledged. There is still much more to learn about the African heritage of the Americas, not only in Yorùbáland and Brazil, but throughout the diaspora, offering us another wide field of research to open for further study.

PART III

Across the Bay of All Saints

Chapter 12

TIMELINE

A Miracle of Memory and Perseverance

Over four million enslaved Africans were taken to Brazil between the mid-1500s to the 1850s; about 44 percent of all Africans forced into the slave trade ended their lives there.[1] For the period ranging from 1801 to 1850, 414,000 Africans arrived in Bahia; it was during this period that Bahia saw a huge upswing in the Nàgó–Yorùbá slave population.[2] According to Eltis: "After 1810 more than half the slaves taken from the Slave Coast[3] to the Americas landed in Bahia."[4]

The shifting demographic of early nineteenth-century Brazil insured the permanent presence of several different African ethnicities or *naçoes*, "nations," in Bahia.[5] In addition to the Nàgó[6] were the JeJe and Angola nations, from Dahomey and Angola, respectively. The Nàgó–Yorùbá had the biggest cultural impact; they were the carriers of traditions of the different kingdoms from which they were born, particularly the peoples from, Kétu, Òyó, Ègbádò, and Ègbá territories. They brought their traditions, customs, culture, and language, and, as emphasized by Dos Santos: "Above all else, they brought to Brazil their religion."[7]

Enslaved members of these principle *naçoes*—Nàgó, Jeje, and Angola, Nàgó being predominant—recreated and maintained cultural systems in Brazil, which became integrated into the complex and rich tradition of Candomblé, an umbrella term for many African-derived initiation lineages. Reconstituted in

Bahia in the early nineteenth century, these traditions grew into a thriving religious practice counting millions of followers throughout Brazil.[8]

The Yorùbá-derived Egúngún cult—the male secret society that venerates and maintains contact with the dead—was one of the West African institutions recreated in Brazil, specifically on the Isle of Itaparica, just across the Baía de Todos os Santos (Bay of All Saints) from the city of Salvador. The island's geographical isolation made it an ideal repository for the knowledge and ritual of the cult; this isolation helped ensure that practitioners remained immune to undue outside influence and retained the purity of knowledge and ritual handed down from their ancestors.

The close-knit family ties and networks on the island contributed to the inheritance of knowledge and tradition. While people did travel back and forth to the mainland by boat, a bridge to the island was built only in 1968, connecting the southern part of the island to a more remote part of mainland Bahia, away from the city of Salvador.[9] Ailton Benedito Sousa, a current resident of Itaparica, told me: "The first bridge to the Isle was built in 1968 called Ponte do Funil (funnel bridge); before that there were two ways to cross, by sailboat—two to three hours with good wind—or, people could take a bus from Salvador to the area where Ponte do Funil now exists and row across the narrow channel."[10]

Isolated by the natural boundaries of water and difficult access, the practice of Egúngún remained protected in family lineages. Even when mainlanders began to vacation on the island in the 1970s, the Egúngún cult remained secretive and closed. This secret society, reborn during slavery in the early part of the nineteenth century, was preserved and thrived unbroken from that early time, through the abolishment of slavery, and into modern times. It has persisted intact and, moreover, the society has grown organically, upholding and adhering to strict ritual protocol as it was initially transmitted through oral tradition.[11]

While protecting themselves from influences of the Portu-
guese-dominated Brazilian society, the Egúngún tradition seems
to have maintained contact with West African practitioners into
the early twentieth century, long after slavery officially ended
in Brazil in 1888. Matory reports "dozens of ships and hundreds
of free Africans traveling from Lagos to Bahia or *through* Bahia
to Rio and Pernambuco between 1855 and 1930s."[12] Free Black
merchants regularly traveled between Bahian and African ports,
a "second migration," exchanging goods and ideas that contributed to African initiation systems in Brazil, including Egúngún.[13]
Further documenting returning travel, Robin Law states: "Large-
scale repatriation of ex-slaves from Brazil seems, however, to
have begun only in the aftermath of the great Bahia slave-revolt
of 1835, when the Bahia authorities deported many ex-slaves
back to Africa."[14] Intercontinental travel by freed slaves, who
had purchased their manumission or were otherwise freed,
was not uncommon even in the midst of slavery; such travelers
surely included practitioners who would affirm their knowledge
and bring back additional *assentos*[15] of Egúngún, augmenting
and enriching their initial source.[16] As a sign of intense cultural
exchange with Africa, there is evidence of a Bahian Egúngún
traveling back to Africa in the nineteenth century: a photo of the
Bambogshe Martins House (which houses an Egúngún shrine), in
Lagos, Nigeria, depicts the "*Songo Egúngún Masquerade* brought
from Bahia, Brazil, to Lagos Nigeria, in the late 19th century."[17]

On Itaparica, the Egúngún cult was sustained by a small group
of networked families, until being consolidated in the terreiro
of the brothers of the Daniel de Paula family, Pedro, Eduardo,
and Olegário. Mariano and Dos Santos outlined a genealogy
of the founders and preservers of the Egúngún cult. Based on
these sources, I present an Egúngún timeline, from the alágbàs
who reconstituted the cult and kept the terreiros functioning and
prospering, to the newly sanctified, immortalized Babá Egúns
of recent generations of Brazilian origin.[18]

EGÚNGÚN ON ITAPARICA ISLAND: 1820–1980

Two lineages of Brazilian Egúngún lead directly back to Africa. The first is the Serafim Teixera Barbosa line, named after Tio Serafim (Uncle Serafim), a former slave, born in Africa. Tio Serafim established the earliest Egúngún terreiro in Brazil—Terreiro Vera Cruz (true cross) ca. 1820, in the Village of Vera Cruz on the island of Itaparica. According to Tio Serafim's grandchildren, Babá Bakábaká and Babá Agboulá, the first "Égun-kings" to be invoked, were born there.

Around 1830, in the village of Mocambo, Marcos Teodoro Pimentel—also known as Marcos-the-Elder—established the Terreiro do Mocambo. Marcos-the-Elder, also an enslaved African, bought himself out of bondage. The term *mocambo* means "fugitive community" or "hide-out," but here it also names a plantation or estate, with a large number of enslaved Africans.[19] Marcos and his son, Tio Marcos, returned to Africa and, during an extended stay of several years, perfected their ritual knowledge of Egúngún. As Tio Marcos was initiated into the secrets of the cult there, they acquired a profound knowledge of Egúngún from the source. Returning to Brazil, they brought with them the assento of Babá Olúkòtún, considered to be the supreme Égun—*Olórí Egum*.[20]

Around 1850 Tio Marcos would go on to found the Tuntum Olúkòtún Terreiro in what was known at that time as Tuntum Village, an old African settlement, now known as Barro Branco (meaning "white clay"), in the area of Ponta da Areia (point of sand).[21] They installed the assento of Babá Olúkòtún, establishing his worship there. Many prominent Ojés were part of Ilê Olúkòtún and this terreiro provided a strong base of knowledge for future terreiros before closing, around 1935, with the death of Tio Marcos.

Around 1840 a son of Tio Serafim, João Dois Metres—so named because of his height—founded the Encarnação Terreiro in the village of Encarnação.[22] Also heading the temple was an African named João Capa-Bode, who transferred the cult of Babá Agboulá—considered one of the patriarchs of the Yorùbá—from Vera Cruz. Babá Agboulá became the terreiro's patron Égun. Terreiro Encarnação closed in the 1930s.[23]

A CONSOLIDATION

Between 1900 and 1920, after many years of studying, working, and participating at the different terreiros on the island, three brothers of the Daniel de Paula family—Pedro, Eduardo, and Olegário—opened their own temple, Terreiro Dos Irmãos Daniel de Paula. The brothers moved the shrines of all the different Babá Éguns from the various terreiros that had become defunct. This move consolidated Egúngún practice in Brazil, establishing the Daniel de Paula family as both the core of Egúngún heritage and as propagators of the tradition.

The patriarch of the family was Manoel Antônio Daniel de Paula, father to the three brothers, who established, preserved, and solidified Egúngún practice on Itaparica Island. The brothers were born during slavery; Manoel and his wife were farmers, and the grandchildren of Africans. Manoel was the *Ojé Baxorum* in the Terreiro Tuntum Olúkọ̀tún, which Tio Marcos founded and where he was the *alapini* (the head of all Egúngún adherents). There, Manoel helped initiate his sons, Pedro, Eduardo, and Olegário (although some believe that Eduardo was initiated elsewhere). The brothers had learned from the terreiros of their uncles, spread across the island in Mocambo, Tuntum, Vera Cruz, and Encarnaçao. When establishing their terreiro, they moved the shrines of all the different Babá Éguns from the various defunct terreiros. The Daniel de Paula terreiro laid the groundwork for the eventual establishment of the now famous Ilê Agboulá, after an intermediate incarnation as Terreiro Barro Vermelho ("red clay"). According to Mariano:

By going to the Terreiros of these uncles (Tio Marcos, Marcos-the-elder, Tio Serafim, and Tio João-Dois-Metres), the brothers Pedro, Eduardo, and Olegário learned the fundamentals of the cult of Babá Olúkòtún—the supreme Égun, both in Africa and Brazil—Babá Bakábaká, and Babá Agboulá.[24]

Finally, they decided to establish their own terreiro between 1900 and 1920. The head of the terreiro was the eldest brother, Eduardo. There, Pedro received the prestigious post of *alapini* from Babá Agboulá. Because Ponta de Areia was largely unpopulated back then, they founded the terreiro there, near the beach, on a spot that is now between the rear of Nossa Senhora das Candeis Chapel and the mangrove swamp. It was very plain, but it had everything they needed. Because the three brothers took their religion very seriously, their terreiro's fame spread and began to attract people from other parts.[25]

With the establishment of their own terreiro in Ponta da Areia, the de Paulas gained great fame through the seriousness of their belief and their ability to help others. The alágbà was the eldest brother, Eduardo. Pedro, the *alapini*, was given this prestigious title by Babá Agboulá. They had consolidated all the ritual knowledge of the "uncles" of the other terreiros and, most importantly, transferred the assentos—the core of sacred objects, tools, and symbols relevant to the individual Éguns.

As the population of Ponta de Areia grew, more outsiders appeared near the barracão, and a singular event caused the decision to move the terreiro again. On June 19, 1940, the police arrested alágbà Eduardo—aged ninety-six at the time and not in good health—along with his wife, Margarida da Conceição. The police had been searching for Antonio, Eduardo's son, after a neighbor had called the police over a simple argument they had had with him. The police never found Antonio, and instead arrested Eduardo and his wife, making a thorough search of the site. This search invaded the sanctity of the terreiro; the police broke sacred objects, viewed secret objects, and trespassed where they had no business. They confiscated some ritual items and brought Eduardo and Margarida to prison in Salvador. Thus, under the guise of ostensibly searching for a culprit involved in an argument, the arrest of Eduardo and Margarida was likely informed by intolerance and prejudice, an attack on their practice of the traditional religion.

The Salvadoran newspaper, *A Tarde,* praised the police for the work and inflated the story to describe complaints from "residents of *Amoreiras* against that terreiro, which was constantly disturbing the peace."[26] It became clear to the cult members that the terreiro must be moved, for "even some new houses were showing up near the *barracão de Babá*."[27]

Thus, in 1940 Pedro, Eduardo, and Olegário relocated the temple to the area of Barro Vermelho in Ponta da Areia, renaming it Terreiro do Barro Vermelho. The patron Égun was Babá Bakábaká. Around 1950 Olegário founded the Terreiro Ilê Oya in honor of his Iansã. In 1958 he left with his son Tolentino (Roxhino) and established Egúngún worship there on the island, reinstating the cult of Olúkòtún. Babá Olúkòtún thus became the patron Babá Égun of Ilê Oya.

Eduardo and his son went on to establish Ilê Agboulá in 1964, yet Dos Santos and others claim it was established in the first quarter of the twentieth century.[28] This Ilê became the direct caretaker and progenitor of the knowledge and tradition stemming from the Terreiro dos Irmãos Daniel de Paula from 1900–1920. The founding of Ilê Agboulá took place as follows, according to Mariano:

Out of gratitude to Babá Agboulá, *ialorixa* Maria Bibiana do Espirito Santo, *Mae* Senhora of Ilê Axé Opô Afonjá, purchased and donated the land to the Égum that became its patron. Àlejò Eduardo and his son Antonio were responsible for removing the shrines of the Éguns from the Barro Vermelho *terreiro* to Bela

Vista (the new location in Ponta de Areia), and Deoscóredes Max-
imiliano dos Santos, better known as *mestre* Didi, the son of *Mae*
Senhora, received the post of *alapini* from Babá Agboulá.[29]

This timeline brings us to ca. 1970–1980, when very few houses
remained that retained the knowledge, wisdom, and ritual of the
Egúngún tradition, or possessed and maintained the assentos
that house the Babá Éguns. Concerning this period, Dos Santos
has observed:

> Their direct descendants, and others whom they initiated in the
> old cult houses, continued to practice the rituals of the cult, and
> preserved to the present day two cult-houses of the Egúngún,
> which are the only existing in Brazil. The Ilê-Agboulá on the
> island of Itaparica was founded during the first quarter of this
> [twentieth] century and can be traced in a direct line from the
> old terreiros. The Ilê Qya is much more recent and it is merely a
> branch of the former.[30]

Ilê Agboulá and the Daniel de Paula family are still considered
the sustaining terreiro from this era, which has carried on the
tradition from the ancient terreiros first established by Marcos the
Elder and Tio Serafim. All Egúngún knowledge was consolidated
here and now represents, along with Ilha Itaparica itself, the
matrix for Egúngún from which other temples are established.[31]

Figure 12.1 outlines the genealogy of Egúngún terreiros. This
figure provides a broad visual picture, given that Itaparica is a
very small island and the participating families worked together
here to insure the survival of the cult.

The history of Egúngún practice on Itaparica is one of constant overlap and group participation, peppered with internal
differences, typical of any structured organization. The growth
of this practice demonstrates cultural resistance, since traditional
religions were outlawed. Sometimes the terreiros were destroyed,

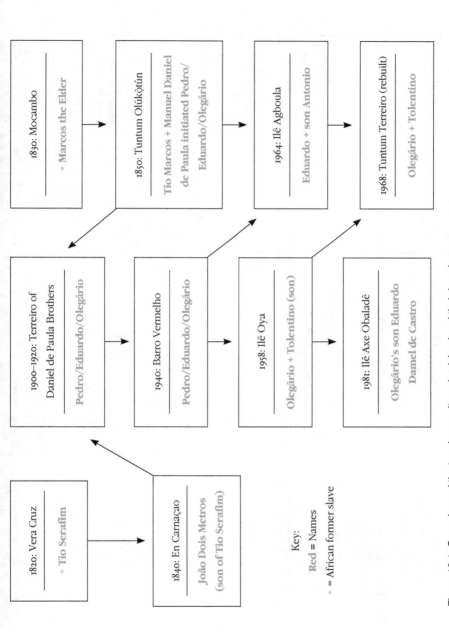

Figure 12.1. Genealogy of the terreiros on Itaparica Island and their founders.

1830: Mocambo
Marcos the Elder

1850: Tuntum Olúkòtún
Tio Marcos + Manuel Daniel
de Paula initiated Pedro/
Eduardo/Olegário

1964: Ilê Agboula
Eduardo + son Antonio

1968: Tuntum Terreiro (rebuilt)
Olegário + Tolentino

1900–1920: Terreiro of Daniel de Paula Brothers
Pedro/Eduardo/Olegário

1940: Barro Vermelho
Pedro/Eduardo/Olegário

1958: Ilê Oya
Olegário + Tolentino (son)

1981: Ilê Axe Obaladê
Olegário's son Eduardo
Damel de Castro

1820: Vera Cruz
Tio Serafim

1840: En Carnação
João Dois Metros
(son of Tio Serafim)

Key:
Red = Names
● = African former slave

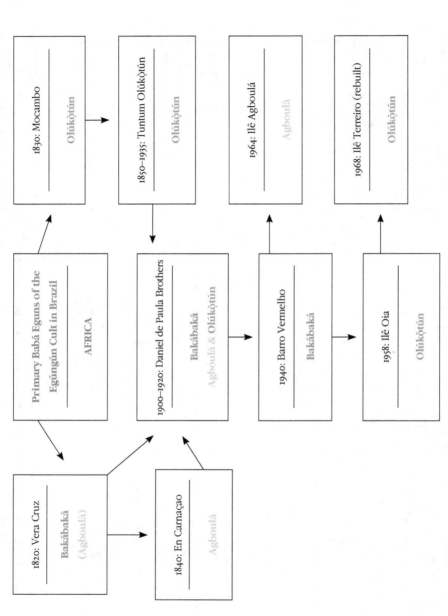

Figure 12.2. Primary Eguns and their migrations.

and criminal charges brought to their leaders, as in the aforementioned case of Eduardo and his wife Margarida in 1940.

Figure 12.2 charts the course of the primary patron Éguns as they moved with the birth and death of terreiros, Babás Bakábaká, Agboulá, and Olúkòtún. As people moved, the terreiros moved, the spirits moved. It should not be thought that these individuals were the only Éguns worshipped—or that any kind of exclusivity existed—only that these particular Éguns functioned as the patrons of particular terreiros.

As a living cultural practice, the Egúngún cult venerates not only the fundamental Babá Éguns shown above, but has also immortalized recently deceased Ojés along with other persons deemed worthy to become Babá Égun. This has augmented and expanded the ancestral pantheon. Figure 12.3 presents a genealogical outline of the members of the Daniel de Paula lineage who received a ceremony as Babá Egúngún.

This lineage depicts the Éguns and their descendants who kept the cult alive, ensuring its perpetuation by performing the necessary rituals for the exaltation of founding elder Ojés as Babá Égun themselves. The three founding brothers, Pedro, Eduardo, and Olegário, now deceased and immortalized as Babá Égun, are venerated, evoked, and brought back to *ilê aiê* in all their due magnificence, love, and exaltation. Now functioning as Babá Egúngún, they have joined the very same Babá Éguns they venerated in their lifetime. The following are brief biographies of each:

- Pedro Daniel de Paula (1889–1949), now *Babá Alatèòrun*. Pedro was *de Xangô Ogodô*, a son of Xangô with the road of Ogodô. He was given the revered title of *alapini*[32] from Babá Agboulá at the brothers' terreiro.
- Eduardo, now *Babá Obaerin*. Eduardo (1844–?) was *de Xangô* (son of Xangô) and the alágbà of Ilê Agboulá. *Babá Obaerin* is the patron Égun of Ilê Obaerin in Recife.

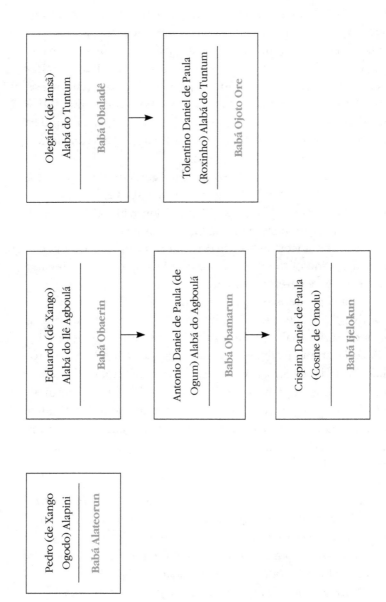

Figure 12.3. Daniel de Paula family members, now Babá Égun.

- Olegário (1882–1971), now *Babá Obaladê*, was de Iansã (son of Iansã)—Qwa and the alágbà of Terreiro Tuntum. He is the patron Égun of Ilê Axé Obaladê.

Figure 12.3 outlines the genealogy of the members of the Daniel de Paula family who are deceased and became Babá Égun, including the second and third generations.

This genealogy to 1980 provides a structural backdrop to the history of Egúngún in Brazil. Around 1980 it was thought that only two functioning terreiros existed in all of Brazil, Ilê Oyá and Ilê Agboulá (there is some difference of opinion here).[33]

This fact should give us pause, because this knowledge and practice of Egúngún survived only through miraculous effort and perseverance, given that since the days of slavery it has remained a completely oral tradition; everything was taught from memory. From the birth of Egúngún in Brazil ca. 1820 to the official abolishment of slavery in 1888 transpires at least sixty-eight years of practice, or three generations. The recreating or reconstitution of Egúngún and its maintenance represents a communal effort of sheer African genius, given the complexity of this practice: what plants were available? What materials were used for the assentos? Where would one procure the valuable cloth to sew the sacred clothes? How much persecution would an enslaved African or his descendants have faced to practice their heritage? While the Brazilian slave markets viciously broke apart families, the Egúngún practitioners of Itaparica held on to the memory of the ancestors, a continual act of resistance against forgetting, resistance against the cultural imposition of the European enslavers. The level of will power and commitment necessary to reconstitute such a profound and complex system of thought and ritual—particularly during the pulverizing brutality of slavery—is now hard to fathom. But the miracle took place, and the family-destroying institution of slavery was unable to destroy this most important link to the families of heaven, our immortal ancestors.[34]

To bring our geneology into present times and location in Rio, today there exist important, authorized terreiros outside of Ilha Itaparica, in Rio de Janeiro—my terreiro, Xangô Cá Te Espero—and in Recife, Ilê Obaerin. In addition, there are terreiros in Salvador, on mainland Bahia. All are direct extensions of a single lineage born from two former slaves as shown in figure 12.1. (As noted, members from both Recife and Ilha Itaparica were present at my Amuxian ceremony.) This is a self-sustaining, cooperative cult.

The pioneering migration of Egúngún to Rio de Janeiro, in the neighborhood of Jacarepaguá, taking the name Terreiro Xango Cá Te Espero, was accomplished by Babá Carlos's mother, Aildés Batista Lopes in 1972. Thompson praises her as a significant figure in the history of Candomblé and Egúngún in Brazil: "Aildés Batista Lopes (1941–1991) was from Bahia where she was steeped in the lore of the founding Candomblés. In fact, such was the depth and prestige of her erudition that she was one of the few persons off the island of Itaparica authorized to maintain a full worship of the masked ancestors (*awon Egúngún*). She died in 1991, an incomparable loss to African–Brazilian studies."[35] In the following chapter, Babá Carlos relates the story of his family coming to Rio, his mother establishing the terreiro of Xango Cá Te Espero, and the "seating" of Babá Ọ̀lọ́jadé, bringing our genealogy of Egúngún into contemporary times and locale.

Chapter 13

"AND THEN THERE WAS THE LETTER"

In my first formal interview with Babá Carlos in April 2016, I asked Babá how Egúngún practice came to Rio de Janeiro. Babá Carlos's response conveyed his own story and that of his mother, Aildés.

Babá Carlos: My mother was initiated soon after she was born. She was born on November 11, 1941 and on May 1, 1942, as a young child, she was initiated.

BW: Which Òrìṣà?

Babá Carlos: She was initiated to Ọya with Oxumarê, and she was already involved spiritually with Candomblé within her family. The religious training and involvement was a heritage from my grandfather, her father. My grandfather Claudio died when my mother was two; there was a large age gap between his and my grandmother's age; he was a much older man. My grandmother was amongst the girls that had been promised to a benefactor—it was not unusual during that time for a younger woman to be promised to a benefactor; it was a normal thing. He was a Navy officer, affording him a much higher social status. My grandmother's father was a menial worker, so she had been promised to him. When he married my grandmother he was almost sixty.

My grandfather Claudio Batista Lopes was the *Ogan*[1] of Oxalá [Ọbàtálá]. My mother was initiated in Ilê Axé Opô Afonjá.

As the years went by, though very involved with Candomblé, my mother did not want to open a terreiro; she was annoyed with certain people and wasn't interested. After my grandmother died my mother got very upset with this particular woman and left Afonjá; she was then welcomed by the people of Terreiro Viva Deus. This was a terreiro of the Angolan tradition, which comes from Tia Maria Neném [Maria Genoveva do Bonfim, 1865–1945]; she was precursor and matriarch of the Angola tradition. Maria Neném was the person who disseminated the Bantu culture, so much so that all the traditional Angolan terreiros, Bate Folha, Tumba Junçara, Viva Deus, Tumbeici, they all come from Maria Neném.

Though my mother didn't want to open a terreiro, many people would come to her for guidance and to perform their obrigação. Every time someone came looking for her to do an obrigação, she would see the person's Òrìṣà and advise them as such. If it was from Angola, if it was Kétu, if it was Jeje [these are the three major naçiones (nations) of Candomblé], she would see it and then she would refer them to the appropriate terreiro. She ended up being a mãe pequena [little mother, ìyá kékeré (Y)] which was a kind of a godmother. She had become the mãe pequena of the people, until her calling concerning Babá Égum [P].

Then, around 1968, Babá Obaerin—the Egúngún of Eduardo Daniel de Paula—from the Agboulá terreiro, summoned my mother and said Ṣàngó was looking for her. Ṣàngó was the patron Òrìṣà associated with our family for six or seven generations. Ṣàngó was our patriarch Òrìṣà, so whenever the next new generation embraced life, they would have to embrace Ṣàngó as well.

This was something that had been seen by my grandfather way back then, even though my mother was only two when he died!

But he had left a letter for me.

This letter was only to come to my knowledge when I was seventeen years old and had been initiated in the Égum cult. By this time I had been made an Ojé. My grandmother was instructed that she could only give me the letter after I became Ojé—initiated in the cult of Egúngún—only then could I receive it.

It's funny how they used to write letters during those times. The discovery of the letter started like this: my grandmother found the letter in a bag, which was inside a bag; the letter was in there also. Now, my mother gave birth to me when she was sixteen. She was two when her father died, she gave birth fourteen years later, and then seventeen more years had gone by. I was now seventeen—*so it had been thirty-one years since this letter had been written.*

When my grandmother gave me the letter, she said:

"There is a letter from your grandfather for you."

I said: "You're kidding, no?"

Then she said she had found it among her things, and when I took it, it looked very old, the paper had yellowed by the effect of time. Now as I am remembering it, it's as if I am looking at the letter right now.

My grandfather wrote:

"My grandson," he wrote, "I leave you these poorly written lines," which was the way one wrote in those days, "by this time you should have just been initiated, and you should be between seventeen and twenty years old. You should already be Ogan of Obaluayê [*Babàlúaíyé* (Y)—father-lord of the world], including being the top priest of the house of Obaluayê, which is Asobá.[2] [Obaluayê is also known as Omolu.]

Translator: and you were already?

Babá Carlos: I was.

Then he instructed me that I was to look for a certain person in Salvador, Tio [uncle] Ajabá, there on the island of Itaparica, in a place called Santo Amaro. I had to look for this person, Uncle Ajabá, in Santo Amaro, not Santo Amaro da Purificação, but Santo Amaro, on the island of Itaparica. There was a map in the letter to look for Tio Ajabá, and a drawing of where this place roughly was located, because he knew the letter would have been given to his grandson only after a long period of time, and the place would have changed. I thought to myself: "this can't possibly exist anymore," but I went there to check it out, and when I got there, it was true—everything had changed, but the drawing of the place, a small farm, was perfect.

I was beginning to feel startled and anxious. There was a password, a phrase I was supposed to say when I knocked at the door; to whoever answered the door, I would say: "I'm Claudio's grandson and I'm here for Tio Ajabá."

And so, I arrived. When I knocked on the door, a lady came to the door—she was very old—when she opened the door I said the words as the letter had instructed:

"I'm Claudio's grandson and I came looking for Tio Ajabá."

Then she smiled. She started to turn to speak—there was a little hallway behind her, it was a just small house with a small porch—and all of sudden someone appeared behind her, very old and very hunched.

He said: "Marica, tell Claudio's grandson to come in."

Then I just fell apart. I broke down upon hearing these words after holding on to this old letter that my grandfather had communicated from so long ago. And when I got nearer to him, he said,

"Claudio's grandson, I've been waiting for you, so I may die."

How does one say he has been waiting for you to die? And how does one react to hearing such a thing?

"You're probably a full Ogan and you should have just finished doing your obligation for Ojé."

And then he said, "I arranged with your grandfather Claudio that I'd die only after I initiated you in the Abará cult which is a branch of Bará Vodou."

Then I relaxed a bit, and he explained more things to me. We went inside and he asked me to sit down, and we started to talk. He explained that he had been initiated both in Égum and Abará cults by my grandfather Claudio, that my grandfather had taken part in his initiation.

My grandfather was a member of both Babá Égum and Bará Vodou.

And there was another surprising aspect to my visit. Here's the part that really interests me a lot, because of the whole situation with Ṣàngó Funké: I learned to identify and to find Ṣàngó Funké, because of what I learned there from Tia Marica. I had learned enough—from this lady whose name was Maria Eugenia do Espírito Santo, called Tia Marica. She was the last priestess of the Gẹ̀lẹ̀dẹ̀ cult and held the title of Ìyá Erelú.

It was there, at that moment of leaving Tio Ajabá's house, that Tia Marica told me: "I'm going to die happy because I'm going to be able to pass on a little of the Gẹ̀lẹ̀dẹ̀ culture to a man; it should have been to a woman, but I'm happy even though it's to a man."

It was because of this, so much so; it's exactly because of what she taught me that that I can deal with the spirit of Ṣàngó Funké. Because I was a man, normally I couldn't receive this knowledge [the Gẹ̀lẹ̀dẹ̀ cult is a female society]. Tia Marica was the Ìyá Erelú; this is the highest title of the Gẹ̀lẹ̀dẹ̀ cult.

Translator: this was her title, or what she gave to you?

Babá: no, it was hers. Which is one of the Oxum's titles, of the Òrìṣà Oxum [P], Ọ̀ṣun [Y]. Oxum is the matriarch of the Gẹ̀lẹ̀dè. There are three main Òrìṣà in Gẹ̀lẹ̀dè: Oxum, Yemonjá, and Obá, but the leader is Oxum. Similarly is Ọya, who is the matriarch in the Égum cult. Oxum is Ìyá Erelú in Gẹ̀lẹ̀dẹ̀, the highest rank in the hierarchy. [This is the title of the Òrìṣà and also the highest human title.]

So, how do I know about Gẹ̀lẹ̀dẹ̀? Because of Tia Marica, that sweet old lady, who was already eighty years old.

Translator: She was the last person who had this knowledge.

Babá Carlos: Yes, who "did" Gẹ̀lẹ̀dẹ̀, that is, who practiced and worshipped Gẹ̀lẹ̀dẹ̀, literally.

[Babá Carlos continues, now discussing the history of the terreiro.] I talked about the arrival in Rio and the establishment of our terreiro Xangô Cá Te Espero in 1972. This was in accordance to what my grandfather had seen, who was the sixth generation of worshipping Ṣàngó; the seventh, my mother's, was already settled, and we are now the eighth generation that we worship Ṣàngó. Every year is ruled by an *odù* [a divinatory pattern or signal] and one or more Òrìṣàs of a particular *odù*. When the Axé [terreiro] was created, it was in a year ruled by *alafia*, a sign that expresses peace and harmony, and it was ruled by the sixteen Oxalás [Oxalá (P), Ọbàtálá (Y) is the father creator figure; he signifies all things white, pure, tranquil, and harmonious]. Alafia rules the year that we have now reached eight generations. And the spirits that at the time were alive in the family are all now here.

BW: Babá, how is it that you became fluent in Yorùbá?

Babá Carlos: In 1964 my mother participated in the first class of Yorùbá offered at the Universidade Federale do Bahia. This course was designed by the leading people of Bahia: Jorge Amado, Caribé, Vivaldo Sinval, Costa Lima, Mestre Didi, Juana, Juanita. So since around that time I was exposed to and started learning Yorùbá. I never took Yorùbá classes though.

I would organize all of my mother's materials; she didn't have time with work and everything else. She didn't have time to organize, and since I was crazy about Babá Égum and Candomblé, this was the opportunity to learn the original language of our tradition. It was there, at home, that I learned Yorùbá.

It was then that I started to organize all the materials, because everything was in the form of handouts and booklets. I still have some surviving booklets; I keep them like relics. I'd organize all the materials to help my mother and she started to stand out as a student because she was able to read. She'd always try to gain more knowledge. At the time the course was taught by Ebenezer Latunde Lasebikan, a Nigerian.[3]

And then I started to study Yorùbá together with her, and at the same time progressed with Egúngún also, because the practice inside the Égum terreiro was a common part of our lives. I had a real thirst for knowledge at a very young age.

It's funny, about four years ago, I went to Salvador, in the neighborhood of Liberdade, the largest Black neighborhood in Latin America, second only to Brooklyn. Ah, and it was hellish hot—it was 1:00 in the afternoon in the summer; I was buying religious items. Then we stopped by a fabric store owned by an African. I looked around, there was only the guy and a female employee. I saw a white container with ice and water. So, feeling that hellish heat, I looked at the young guy who was a "filho de santo" [son of the saint] of Terreiro Afonjá, and spoke to him in Yorùbá that it was very hot and I wanted to drink some ice-cold water. And the African man understood; surprised, he jumped up and said: "Where did you learn to speak Yorùbá?" I asked: "Do you find it strange that I speak Yorùbá here in Bahia?" He answered: "I'm used to subbing for many Yorùbá teachers here and people have a very hard time to learn it here in Brazil." Because Yorùbá is tonal; you have the same word, the same spelling, only the tonal stress changes, and a word can mean many things. For instance: *ehin* may be *back*, *teeth*, or *egg*, depending on the tonal position. And he was intrigued at my speaking Yorùbá with so much fluency. Then I said: "Ah, the secret is in the House of Babá Agboulá, in the Égum terreiro, where I practiced a lot and studied." I had a knack for it, absorbing the language.

As I said before, around 1968 my mother was summoned to the terreiro to receive a message from Şàngó through Egúngún Obaerin. So it was then, in 1970, combined with a career opportunity that we came to Rio to live for good. Before that it was only for vacation. Then in 1972 we founded the terreiro here.

When I was ten years old I became Amuxian; I was initiated on Itaparica, the year was 1967. We came here in 1970; I was thirteen. I was already like you, Brian [addressing the author], I was Amuxian. I was about to be initiated as Ojé. I became Ojé in 1974, forty-two years ago. I lived sequestered, the stuff of family, right? I was son of Dona Didi [Aildés], my mother. So I was my mother's son; my mother demanded from me more than what she'd demand from any other person, I had to be the best among the best.

[Babá and I go back and forth with my basic Portuguese to clarify.]

Babá: No, I was already like you, I was Amuxian.

There is a book there tells the story of my whole family, Antonio Daniel de Paula, Eduardo Daniel de Paula, my alagbá's father. It speaks about this family of the people who brought Babá Égum from Bahia, which started on Itaparica Island. The first Égum to be invoked here in Brazil was Babá Bakábaká, who is an Obaluaiye Égum, an Omolu. And later other ancestors were brought here to Brazil. Before the terreiro of Babá Agboulá, other terreiros were created. The Agboulá terreiro is from the same year I was born, 1957. I'm fifty-eight years old.

Translator (getting bewildered at us trying to communicate): Guys, how have you communicated so far?

Babá and myself (laughing): Somewhat in Portuguese, somewhat in Yorùbá, somewhat in, *everything* . . . !

Babá Carlos: But it takes many years for him [the author] to learn; there are many things for us to talk about but sometimes the wires get crossed. But when a ritual is going on, he is able to better participate.

And he came because it was the spirit of his godmother, of his *mãe de santo*, Ṣàngó Funké, who talked to him in the United States, who came with him to Brazil. You're in her homeland; now she has the means to communicate with you.

[Now turning to the subject of the patron Babá Égun of his terreiro, Babá Ọlọ́jadé]

Babá Carlos: Babá Ọlọ́jadé is not my direct ancestor. When I carried out my obligations with Babá Obaerin and Babá Alapalá, Babá Obaerin became in charge of our terreiro; it was he who brought all the messages. They said that an entity would have to be brought from Africa that was waiting for me to be born in order for him to be worshipped. He was being brought from

Figure 13.1. Our translator, Brazilian actress Viviane Porto, Babá Carlos, and the author during our first interview.

Africa. He was an African king. Africa had fifty nations that were smaller than Madureira [a small area in Rio]; he was the king of one of those nations. Because his family was betrayed and there were no descendants left to worship him, Babá Obaerin and Babá Alapalá brought him, and he had said that the priest who would take care of him would be born in Brazil and in the family of Babá Alapalá, and would be a son of Ṣàngó's family. And so he arrived. And then, in 1979 I was awarded with the gift of Babá Ọ̀lọ́jadé's arrival. Babá Obaerin ordered his son, Antonio Daniel de Paula, who was alive at the time, my alagbá, to install the Égum of Babá Ọ̀lọ́jadé at our terreiro in Rio.

My alagbá, Antonio, said: "Get used to this name because he's going to take care of you. Ọ̀lọ́jadé. Ọ̀lọ́jadé. Ọ̀lọ́jadé. *The master of the market.*"

It was said that in addition to worshipping the Òrìṣà, to worshipping Ṣàngó, one needed to worship Babá Égum as well.

Babá Obaerin was the spirit of Eduardo Daniel de Paula who ordered his flesh and blood son Antonio Daniel de Paula, who is my alagbá, to come to prepare the things related to Babá Égum. This was a great honor, so I'm very proud that it wasn't me who prepared things here; it was he who prepared my Égum, my *lesa-yin* [the sacred Égum room], my house of Ilê Ibó. This included my alagbá, Antonio Daniel de Paula, together with Mestre Didi, the alapini [the head of all the Egúngún worshippers in Brazil], and Antonio's son, Cosme Daniel de Paula. The Antonio Daniel de Paula we are speaking of today is no longer living, he is now an Egúngún himself, Babá Obamarun; and Antonio's son, Cosme Daniel de Paula, he is also now Egúngún, Babá Ijelokun.

Bàbá àwá ti dìmulẹ̀
Wọn ti digi àlóyè,
Èyí tí ò leè kú mó,
Èso wẹẹrẹ ni wón ń so.

Our father is now an ancestor in whom to confide.
He is a transplanted tree that thrives,
A tree that never dies,
But bears countless fruits.[4]

Chapter 14

CONCLUSION

The Egúngún cult is among the most significant spiritual heritages existing in the African diaspora in the Americas. Established on the Brazilian island of Itaparica in the early 1800s based on traditions of the Yorùbá in West Africa, the practice has been maintained for over two centuries by a small of group of families. This tradition as practiced in Brazil—a manifestation of oral tradition and miraculous memory—has persevered and proliferated since its reconstitution in the early 1800s on the isolated island of Itaparica.

The existence of Egúngún in contemporary Brazil evidences the cultural resistance of generations of African descendants and their communities, by maintaining symbolic practices that narrate historical ties with Africa that are not based on the condition of slavery. If the educational curriculum of Brazil teaches only that Black Brazilians are descended from slaves, Egúngún practice tells us a different story, that the Yorùbá-speaking people of West Africa had royal families, which are represented by the Egúngún performance in elaborate rituals.

The practice of Egúngún occurs in a unique, localized concept of the microcosmic terreiro, a walled-off property with shrines and buildings that recreate a mythic Africa, where communities of initiates meet in highly organized fashions to cook, talk, dance, and sing in ways related to Afro-Brazilian heritage. During rites, one witnesses virtuosic drumming, astonishing for the sheer volume of the drums echoing ferociously off the concrete walls; the fervent participation of the adherents; the grandiose spectacle of the magnificent dress of Egúngún: spectacularly adorned garments, made of the finest cloths, embroidered with mirrors, sequins, cowrie shells, and feathers in an infinite variety of emblematic decoration; the impossibly acrobatic dance of the Éguns; and finally, the medium with which Égun communicates from beyond the grave: the mystical *eegi*, the sound of the wind blowing through the bamboo grove, the *dancô*, sometimes sounding like the gravel-voiced colobus monkey, sometimes sounding like a high-pitched flute-like whistle, with infinite shades of mystical timbre in between. All these ritual sounds and symbols work to create a sense of the numinous, other-worldly atmosphere where the spectacularly ornamented cloth assemblages of Egúngún represent African and Afro-Brazilian ancestors who have come back to *aiê* once again, to interact, guide, and be in fellowship with the community of living initiates and believers.

We can't remember all of you by name,
nevertheless, we invoke you all.[1]

Our collective ancestors have come to visit, judge, admonish, bless, and clean our lives of negativity, and help and guide us in our destinies. They bring blessings of good health, fertility, prosperity, love, and happiness; we experience deep contentment knowing that those who have left us have not left us. We are able to acknowledge that our intuitive experiences of passed loved ones—in a dream, in a moment of knowing—are instances of real connection, not psychological manifestations based on emotional need. Brazilian initiates have managed to keep this tradition alive and thriving in the diaspora, eventually proliferating and spreading it from the isolated isle of Itaparica to include three major areas in Brazil: Bahia; Rio de Janeiro, and Recife. It has grown in recent years from the diminished existence in the

1970s and '80s of a handful of terreiros to a flourishing practice now being propagated for the future.

The Egúngún society has recently become so popular that current leadership is concerned and dismayed by false claims of membership and initiations by people outside the initiation community. In 2015 a statement was released by the Association of the Terreiros of the Cult of Babá Égun of Bahia and Brazil to affirm the secretive, disciplined, sacred nature of membership in the cult and its initiations.[2]

According to legends within the oral tradition in Brazil and Africa, Egúngún has existed forever, being one of the three great *awo* (mysteries) Olódùmarè bequeathed to man, providing the ability to communicate with lineage ancestors and ancient kings, firmly establishing the knowledge that life continues after death. Through Egúngún practice, loved ones who pass into the other world maintain a firm connection with the living family. Even though they exist in another place, they remain part of the family. Their bodies have returned through *Ọya Bagan* to the womb of mother earth, *Onílẹ̀*, the caretaker and eternal resting place for all. As Morton-Williams so eloquently states: "*Onílẹ̀*, as a symbol of eternity, unity with it is a sharing in endless being.[3] "They are now *ará ọ̀run*, "people of the life beyond."[4]

We don't know why the rituals of Egúngún did not survive in Cuba or the United States. While the rites of Egúngún were recreated exclusively in Brazil in the 1800s by unwilling migrants from West Africa, other aspects of Égun worship were practiced in plantation economies of Cuba, Haiti, Trinidad, and so on.

Prof. Wande Abímbọ́lá theorized that if knowledgeable members of the Egúngún cult had arrived in Cuba in the 1800s, then it could have been established there.[5] Nevertheless, the philosophy and tradition of veneration of and communication with the ancestors continued in the recognition and supplication to lineage ancestors by members of all initiation systems in Cuba—Abakuá, Arará, Congo, and Lukumí—and also through the practice of Kardecian spiritism. It was only in Brazil that the Egúngún society flourished.

But as this study has shown, the re-creation of Egúngún practice has been a continual process by each generation of initiates, on the isle of Itaparica or on mainland Brazil. In the New York area, my own godmother in Santería/Lukumí and traditional Yorùbá practice, Betty Barney, now Ṣàngó Funké, worked to reestablish an Egúngún lineage directly from West Africa. Her mission was to reinstitute an ancestral connection that had been brutally severed, and, in her own words, "to forever break the psychological chains of slavery for the Black person in America." She imagined an enabling consciousness for Black youth in North America who have yet to heal or conquer the effects of perpetual familial destruction, to reconcile the inner turmoil of the subconscious by establishing an incorruptible link to their ancestors, who have the ability to guide and protect, providing an invincible psychological and spiritual stability. She thought that this psychological and spiritual link could bypass centuries of learned behavior and motivate the living with a sense of a rare and cherished, powerful heritage, enabling them to rediscover an African-based identity, to be spiritually restored at the deepest levels. Her idea was that to connect with Egúngún is to know how to live in the most profound sense: *Let them old souls into your heart, Eli. Let them touch you with the hands of time. Let 'em feed your head with a wisdom that ain't from this day and time.*[6]

Within the cult of death lie centuries of collective memory and fathomless spiritual strength.

Se aiyé gún.
Those who make the earth stable.[7]

We need those who make the earth stable.
We need our great-great-great-grandfathers and -grandmothers.

I hope this work will educate and inspire others to continue research and participation in the Egúngún societies, and that some of these words might cause us to pause, individually and collectively, to consider our ancestors once again. To my godfather Ojé Dúdú and all the adherents of Egúngún, my godmother Ṣàngó Funké—who is now *ará ọrun*, and the fisherman families of Itaparica who so carefully and righteously maintained the vision of Egúngún, I salute you.

GLOSSARY

P = Portuguese
Y = Yorùbá

abala—literally, cloth—cloth of Egúngún, see *aṣọ*.

abian or abiã—A novice or candidate for initiation in Candomblé.

abô—A bath of sacred leaves employed for medicinal, spiritual, or magical ends. Essential to the initiation process. Also known as *banho de folhas, banho de desenvolvimento, banho de descarga,* and *amaci* (P).

agô (P), àgò (Y)—asking permission to make way, to enter.

"Aiyé lojá, orun nilé"—"the physical world is a marketplace, the otherworld (heaven) is our home."

alágbà—The head of an Egúngún house. In Nigeria, Alágbàá is a hereditary chief who heads the Egúngún society.[1]

Alapini—The head of the entire Egúngún cult in Brazil.

Amuxian (P), amúìṣan (Y)—Attendant to Egúngún, the bearer of the *ixan* (iṣan [Y]) ("switch or branch": see ixan), the first of the two levels of initiation into the Egúngún priesthood in Brazil.

àpá (Y)—multicolored appliqué panels that are part of Egúngún's assemblage.

aparaká (P)—undeveloped spirit, intermediate stage for a spirit who is to become Egúngún.

ará òrun—referring to ancestral spirits: people of heaven or people from a distant place.

aṣe (Y), axé (P)—sacred, vital force or energy of the Yorùbá and Candomblé, which is concentrated in initiates and rituals. Axé (P) can also be used to denote terreiro.

aṣọ (Y), axo (P)—clothing, (outfit, cloth assemblage, costume), of Egúngún. Also opá (P) and èkú (Y).

assento, assentamento—the consecrated physical abode, or "seat," of Babá Égun.

atabaque—sacred drums of Candomblé.

atọ́kùn—an assistant to the Egúngún cult; (Y), same as Amuxian (P).

àtòrì (Y)—(*glyphaea lateriflora*) the tree from which the iṣan whips are made to control Egúngún in Yorùbáland. In Brazil, these whips [ìxan (P)] are made from the biriba tree (*rollinia deliciosa*), the same tree used in making the bow of the berimbau.

Àwíṣẹ—a high title in Ifá.

axexê—A funeral ritual in Candomblé.

ayé (Y), aiê (P)—earth, but more so the material world and all that exists on it, as opposed to the invisible spiritual world.

Babá—father (Y); appropriate salutation to a male priest, can also denote an elder Égun.

Babá Égun—elder égun, or simply Babá.

babalaô (P), babaláwo (Y)—Literally "father-of-secrets"; priest of Ifá and diviner. The babaláwo/Ifá tradition did not take hold and continue in Brazil. But now there are many Brazilian babaláwos, as Cuban Ifá priests have been migrating there, and also from Africa.

Babá kekeré—Literally "small father," the second in command in a terreiro.

barracào—A large, main hall or room in the terreiro where all large ceremonies and public functions are held. Literally "barracks," also refers to the slave quarters where they were held.

Caboclo—Indigenous spirit, revered in Candomblé, including the most traditional terreiros of Bahia.

cameiera, or *coluna*—central pole in the middle of a barracào. During ceremony it is decorated with flowers and other accoutrements, the spiritual axis where the axé is focused. See ọ̀pá ọ̀run.

Candomblé—A Yorùbá–derived religion in Brazil dedicated to the orixás. Candomblé is an Angolan-derived term, and early lineages had Kongo content.

Candomblé de Angola—A *nacion* of Candomblé, particularly common in southern Bahia, that incorporates Bantu divinities within the general Yorùbá structure.

centro de mesa—A Kardecist spiritist center, also called *mesa blanca* (literally "white table").

ebo—Sacrificial offering to an Òrìṣà, or a ceremony or work meant to bring about positive change.

ebomi—A terreiro elder, initiated for more than seven years.

ẹ̀bọ́rá—spirit, a generic name for Egúngún.

ẹdun—colobus monkey, central to Egúngún creation myths.

eegi (ṣẹ́gi)—the mode of sound with which Egúngún communicates.

Égun—A spirit of the dead. Can be used generically to reference a single ancestor spirit, or when referring to a spirit who has become a revered ancestor, Egúngún; a diminutive of Egúngún.

Égun Àgbà—elder Égun, "the ancient ones."[2]

Egúngún (Égun, Babá Égun, Babá)—These are all common monikers for an immortalized ancestral spirit venerated in Egúngún temples in Brazil and Africa. Also the name of the cult itself, whose sources are in Yorùbáland, West Africa.

Èhìn Ìwa—afterlife.

equedi—A woman consecrated to a divinity in Candomblé who does not experience trance, but is responsible for caring for initiates in trance, and present at all ritual ceremonies.

èkú—any Egúngún outfit, costume.

Exú (P), Èṣù (Y)—Exu is the messenger Òrìṣà, who communicates with the Òrìṣà and Olódùmarè on behalf of humans and is owner of choice and opener of roads; Òrìṣà of the crossroads of life. In Umbanda, the exú is a disincarnated spirit, not an Òrìṣà.

filha-de-santo—Literally "daughter of the saints." A female Candomblé adherent who has passed through lengthy initiation process. Most of the support work of the terreiro is carried out by the filhas.

filho-de-santo—Literally "son of the saints," the male counterpart of filha-de-santo.

Gèlèdè—female society celebrating the powers of Ìyá won, "our mothers," the all-powerful feminine principle of creation. A balancing counterpart to the all-male Egúngún society.

Iansa/Yansa—(mother-of-nine) an alternative name for Oya. A hot-tempered female Òrìṣà associated with wind, storms, lightning, and the cemetery. Mother of Egúngún.

iaô (P)—new initiate. see ìyàwó (Y).

iború—A ceremony dedicated to the head, sometimes preparatory or preliminary to initiation ritual; a propitiation to one's inner consciousness. Similar in function to the Lukumí *rogacion*.

ìgbàle—sacred Egúngún grove.

Ifá—Yorùbá god of divination whose messages are revealed by the babaláwo priest.

ijímèré—red savannah patas monkey, central to Egúngún creation myths.

Ikú—death.

Ilê Agboulá—famous Egúngún temple on the island of Itaparica from which all other current temples were born, the matrix.

Ilê Axé—Candomblé temple, synonymous with terreiro.

Ilê Axé Opô Afonjá—famous Ilê Axe/Candomblé house or terreiro that prides itself on its connection to African origins.

Ilê Axé Opô Aganju—well-known Candomblé *terreiro* in the Lauro da Frietas area of Bahia, headed by Pae de Santo Balbino Daniel de Paula.

ìlèkè—beads which represent the different Òrìṣà.

ìrokò—West African tree believed to be the residence of the Òrìṣà Ìrokò, god of time. In Brazil, a species of ficus was substituted for the African ìrokò (Y).

ìṣan (Y), ìxan (P)—The slender switch, made in Brazil from the *biriba* tree (*rollinia deliciosa*), that summons and controls the Éguns. In Yorùbáland it is made from the àtòrì tree (*glyphaea lateriflora*). Gleason refers to *ìṣan ni ọpáku,* "death stick."³

Iyalorixá, Ialorixa—A high priestess and head of a Candomblé terreiro, especially in Candomblé de Ketu. Mother-of-the-Òrìṣà, more often known as mãe-de-santo.

Iyamí Oxorongá (P), Ìyàmi Òṣòrònga (Y)—Meaning my-mother, our-mothers. Associated with the Ajé, entities of feminine power of the women's Gẹ̀lẹ̀dẹ̀ society. Erroneously (but commonly) referred to as "witches."

Ìyá awon, Ìyá won—our mothers, mother of all humans.

Ìyá Nlá—The Great Mother, the female principle in nature personified.

Ìyàwó or Iaô—Literally "wife or bride of the Òrìṣà," a Candomblé adherent who has passed through lengthy initiation, i.e., "made Òrìṣà," but still within the seven-year period of training and service. A hierarchical status inferior to the ebomis.

limpeza (P)—A ritual cleansing meant to purify a person or place of negative energies.

mãe-de santo—A high priestess in the terreiro; literally, mother-of-saint, where saint is the synonym of Òrìṣà, a consequence of the Catholic cultural influence in Afro-Brazilian Candomblé.

mãe pequena (P)—Also known in Yorùbá as Ìyá kekeré; literally "small-mother." Assistant of a pai-de-santo or mãe-de-santo. Second in command of the terreiro.

obì àbàtà—four-segment kọla nut used for divination found in Yorùbáland.

obì gbanja—two-segment kọla commonly found in Brazil.

obì kọla (*colá acuminate*) (Y)—a nut used for offerings, to eat, and for divination.

obrigação—literally, "obligation," but more accurately a ritual, ceremony, offering, or sacrifice to the Òrìṣà. The obrigação is performed variously as needed, or at specific times after initiation to mark progress through Candomblé's initiatory grades. Fundamental precepts and liturgy within Candomblé.⁴

Odù—a signal produced by divinatory means using the system of cowrie shells (buzios [P], caracoles [SP], dilogun [Y]) or the system of Ifá. Also, mythical wife of Òrúnmìlà.

Ògún—male Òrìṣà associated with iron, war, and revolution, and having a mythical relationship with Qya. A symbol of strength and resistance, Ògún wields his machete not only to conquer earthly enemies, but also to cut or make a spiritual path, and clear impediments from an adherent's life.

Ojé (P), Òjè (Y)—high priest of the Egúngún cult.

òkú—A dead body.

Olódùmarè—God.

Òlójadé, Babá Òlójadé—king of the Candomblé, Xango Cá Te Espero. The patron Egúngún of this terreiro, owner of the marketplace.

Olúkòtún Olórí Égun—The lord at the right hand of God, the supreme chief of Egúngún.[5]

Onílè—mother earth; a small mound of earth outside ìgbàlè—a fundamental, collective representation of the ancestors.

òpá ikú—Égun stick, used to summon the dead.

òpá òrun—"staff of heaven."

Òrìsàs [Y], Orixas (P), Orichas (Sp.), Orishas (Eng.)—pantheon of deities found in the Yorùbá, Candomblé, and Lukumí and other African diasporic spiritual traditions.

òrun—The Yorùbá spiritual universe as conceived with nine levels of space occupied by the Òrìsà, Olorun, and the spirits of the dead. Considered to be a place of immeasurable and unfathomable vastness. Commonly translated as "heaven," another example of Catholic influence on Candomblé.

Òrúnmìlà—deity of divination, witness to destiny, he-who-sits-at-the-right-hand-of God.

Oxalá (P), Obàtálá (Y)—deity of whiteness and purity, calmness, and tranquility. Father figure of the world.

pai-de-santo—A Candomblé priest and leader of a terreiro.

pai pequeño—The terreiro head's direct assistant. Also known as bàbá kékeré.

roda (P)—circle; in Candomblé, refers to the circle of adherents that dance to the Òrìsàs around the central pole, the *coluna* in the barracão.

ronco—tiny room where initiates spend much of their time in isolation. (Y)

terreiro—Candomblé temple, which usually includes a barracão [barracks], separate rooms (ronco) for initiates, and small individual houses for each of the orixá. Some terreiros house adherents who may live on the site for many years. The term also refers to the community of adherents. Though literally translated as yard or square, poetically it means land, as the temple represents the "African land of the deity," so it's a little piece of Africa.[6]

NOTES

A Note on Orthography

1. For additional information on the Yorùbá language in the diaspora, see Maureen Warner Lewis, *Yorùbá Songs of Trinidad* (Tuscaloosa: University of Alabama Press, 1994), and *Trinidad Yorùbá: From Mother Tongue to Memory* (Tuscaloosa: University of Alabama Press, 1996).

2. Victor Manfredi, "A Note on the Typography," in Phyllis Galembo, *Divine Inspiration: Bénin to Bahia* (New York: Athelia Henrietta Press, 1993), ix.

3. Káyòdé J. Fákinlede, *Beginner's Yorùbá* (New York: Hippocrene Books, 2005), 14.

4. Wande Abímbólá and Ivor Miller, *Ifá Will Mend This Broken World* (Roxbury, MA: Aim Books, 1997). Abímbólá and Miller illuminate many Lukumí diasporic phrases traced to their original Yorùbá.

5. Roy C. Abraham, *Dictionary of Modern Yorùbá* (London: University of London Press, 1958).

6. In some instances, such as proper names in Portuguese, I do not impose the Yorùbá; e.g., the name of the temple Xango Cá Te Espero, or Babá Carlos.

Poem

1. Bade Ajuwon, "Ògún's Ìrèmòjé: A Philosophy of Living and Dying," in *Africa's Ògún: Old World and New*, edited by Sandra Barnes (Bloomington: Indiana University Press, 1997), 194. Ajuwon states: "Death cannot be considered as a finality . . . it is a gateway to another kind of life: the life of an ancestor" . . . "moving from the solemnity of death to the joy of another kind of existence." This poem is from Ìrèmòjé (a body of poetic funeral chants) "instructing the living concerning immortality."

Chapter 1: Introduction: From Long Island to Brazil

1. Chambers Brothers, *Time Has Come Today*, Columbia Records, 1967.

2. Cecil Taylor, *Silent Tongues*, Arista Records, 1975.

3. Katy Roberts, *Live at L'Archipel*, independent release, 2005.

4. Dilogún is the Lukumí term for the sixteen cowrie-shell system of divination practiced by Òrìṣà worshippers in the diaspora. Also known as *caracoles* (SP) and *buzios* (P). From the Yorùbá *ẹẹrìndínlógún*, divination with sixteen cowries. For further information see two enlightening articles, Wande Abímbọ́lá, "The Bag of Wisdom: Ọsun and the Origins of Ifá Divination," in *Ọsun Across the Water: A Yorùbá Goddess in Africa and the Americas*, edited by Joseph M. Murphy and Mei-Mei Sanford (Bloomington: Indiana University Press, 2001), 141–54; and David O. Ogunbile, "Ẹẹrìndínlógún: The Seeing Eyes of Sacred Shells and Stones," in *Ọsun Across the Water*, 189–212.

5. See George Brandon, *Santeria from Africa to the New World: The Dead Sell Memories* (Bloomington: Indiana University Press, 1997), 85–89. "Espiritismo is a variant of spiritism founded in France by Hippolyte Rivail (1804–1869), an engineer who wrote under the pseudonym of Allan Kardec."

6. See David Brown, *Santeria Enthroned: Art, Ritual, and Innovation in an Afro-Cuban Religion* (Chicago: University of Chicago Press, 2003), 62–63.

7. See Allen Kardec, *The Spirit's Book* (New York: Studium, 1980).

8. Thompson noted, "this was very hip of her." Personal communication (2010).

9. There is not necessarily a direct correlation between the two events; though for me it seemed a natural progression. When you receive your ìlẹ̀kẹ̀*s* it causes both an opening and a balancing of the metaphysical bodies. This openness is conducive to accelerating and enhancing mediumistic abilities; I believe it to be so in my case.

10. The term "made ocha" means to be initiated; it is also called "making the saint" in the Latino community. For information pertaining to this ceremony see Brown, *Santeria Enthroned*; Michael Atwood Mason, *Living Santeria: Rituals and Experiences in an Afro-Cuban Religion* (Washington, DC: Smithsonian Books, 2002); and Joseph M. Murphy, *Santería: African Spirits in America* (Boston: Beacon Press, [1988] 1993).

11. Betty Barney, "You're the talk of the Òrìṣà circuit!" Personal communication, 1985.

12. Ifá divination is the complex divinatory system of the Yorùbá. The babaláwo (literally father-of-secrets—the Ifá diviner) uses the òpèlè or *ikin* (palm nuts) to produce one of 256 signals or patterns called *odù*; each *odù* represents a chapter of the Ifá corpus. Each chapter contains countless stories and parables; it is from the odù cast that the diviner will address the client's problem. See William Bascomb, *Ifá Divination:*

Communication between Gods and Men in West Africa (Bloomington: Indiana University Press, 1969).

13. Abímbọ́lá and Miller, *Ifá Will Mend*, 124. Traditional saying when mentioning the dead, like "rest in peace." Abímbọ́lá translates *Ibae, bayén tonu* as Ìbaẹ Ìbaẹ ẹnì tó nù, meaning: I salute you, I salute you, those who have disappeared.

14. Pessoa de Castro states: "Candomblé comes from the Bantu: ka-n-dómb-él-é, 'the action of praying—to ask for by the intercession of the gods.' Thus, Candomblé (P), means worship, praise, prayer, invocation and, by extension, the place where these ceremonies are performed." Yeda Pessoa de Castro, "Religions of African Origin in Brazil: Designations, origins and new and little-known cults" (San Luis de Maranhao, June 1985), 139.

15. *Xango Cá Te Espero* translates literally as: Xango, here we wait for you. A *terreiro* is literally a yard, or square, now commonly understood as a temple in the Candomblé religion. A terreiro is a compound often featuring high enclosing walls. Inside there are individual small houses for each Òrìṣà and a large hall—the barracão—for ceremonies and public events. It is a microcosm of the world; the head priest or priestess lives there and often so do some members of the terreiro.

16. Except for the initiatory events for which I am sworn to secrecy.

17. See Brandon, *Santería from Africa to the New World*; Brown, *Santería Enthroned*; and Mason, *Living Santería*.

18. Drewal and Drewal, "More Powerful Than Each Other."

19. Juana Elbein Dos Santos and Deoscoredes M. Dos Santos, "Ancestor Worship in Bahia," *Journal de la Societe des Americanistes* 58 (1969): 79–108.

20. Juana Elbein Dos Santos, *Os Nágôs e a Morte: Pàde, Àsèsè e o Culto Égun na Bahia* (Petropolis, Brazil: Editora Vozes, 2002). Juana is a well-known acquaintance to Babá Carlos.

21. Agnes Mariano, *Obaràyí* (Salvador, Brazil: Barabô, 2009).

22. Babá Carlos Ojé Dúdú, personal communication in Rio de Janeiro, 2016.

23. See Katherine J. Hagedorn, *Divine Utterances: The Performance of Afro-Cuban Santería* (Washington DC: Smithsonian Books, 2001); Murphy, *Santería*, among others.

24. Several writers of African diasporic traditions were drawn to the religion as a research topic, and subsequently found themselves as participants. (Without the enticement of research would these writers have found Òrìṣà? I believe so.) Karen McCarthy Brown, *Mama Lola: A Vodou Priestess in Brooklyn* (Los Angeles: University of California Press, 1991); Hagedorn, *Divine Utterances*; and Murphy, *Santería*. All are highly recommended.

25. Joseph M. Murphy, *Working the Spirit: Ceremonies of the African Diaspora* (Boston: Beacon Press, 1994), x, xi.

26. Ivor Miller, personal communication, 2019.

27. Thompson, personal communication, 2015.

28. David Eltis and David Richardson, *Atlas of the Transatlantic Slave Trade* (New Haven, CT: Yale University Press, 2010), 159–96, 303. "The transatlantic voyage between Africa and the Americas, *The Middle Passage*, notorious because of the cramped, unhygienic conditions suffered by the slaves below decks, became a key reference point of the anti-slave-trade movement." Eltis and Richardson devote a chapter to this topic.

29. Robert Voeks, *Sacred Leaves of Candomblé: African Magic, Medicine, and Religion in Brazil* (Austin: University of Texas Press, 1997), 148. See also Eltis and Richardson, *Atlas of the Transatlantic Slave Trade*, 203, 303. For a comprehensive account of slave routes and populations between Africa and the Atlantic world, see Part III, 87–158.

30. David Eltis, "The Diaspora of Yorùbá Speakers, 1650–1865: Dimensions and Implications," in Falola and Childs, *The Yorùbá Diaspora*, 28.

31. Eltis, "The Diaspora of Yorùbá Speakers," 28.

32. Mikelle Smith Omari-Tunkara, *Manipulating the Sacred: Yorùbá Art, Ritual, and Resistance in Brazilian Candomblé* (Detroit: Wayne State University Press, 2005), 92.

33. Thompson, personal communication, January 2017.

34. "All ceremonies begin with an '*ayuba*,' a reverence to the dead, extending to the most remote ancestors, those not known personally, 'to those who lived and died in Guiní' (Guinea, West Africa), who even so recognize them and who also, like the closest ones, can intervene in their lives, protect them or bother them"; Lydia Cabrera, *Yemayá y Ochún* (Miami: Ediciones Universal, [1980] 1996), 93–94 (translation, Ivor Miller). This philosophy of acknowledging ancestors remembered or not, known or unknown, is purely African.

35. From a Cuban initiate, as per Miller, personal communication, 2019: "It's true that the cult of Égun or Egúngún is not known in Cuba, but we do have: espiritismo with variants in Santiago de Cuba with its influences from Vodun and ancestors; the Palo Ngangulero works in the cemetery and with spiritual dogs; the Abakuá society has its funerary spirit, Ireme Anamanguin; Ocha has the Olokun mask of the dead. The Égun and funerary rites with bata drums have an Oya dance with a branch of Hierba Paraíso. We also have the altar of Eggun or Zaraza; the chants to Égun and the Òrun ceremony of the babaláwos. That is to say, in Cuba, 'the concept of Égun is foundational to all African-derived initiation systems.'"

36. Robert Farris Thompson and Joseph Cornet, *Four Moments of the Sun: Kongo Art in Two Worlds* (Washington, DC: National Gallery of Art, 1981).

37. Personal communication, Ivor Miller, 2018.

38. Mardi Gras Museum of Costumes and Culture, New Orleans. On a trip to New Orleans in 2017, I noted numerous Mardi Gras outfits with cowrie shell patterns that could have easily been interchangeable with designs found in Egúngún *aṣọ* in Brazil and Nigeria.

39. This initial planting of Egúngún is documented in Adédayò Oló-gundúdú, *The Cradle of Yorùbá Culture* (New York: Institute of Yorùbá Culture, 2008), 6–16. Chief Adédayò mistakenly assigns the date of 1990 to this event, which occurred in 1987.

40. David Brown, personal communication, 2018.

41. The title *Oluwo Pássoro* translates poetically as "*a great protector of Oxala*" (Ọbàtálá [Y]—the Òrìṣà of tranquility and purity). I received this title during the culmination of my first ceremonial visit to the terreiro in 2008, from the king of the Egúngún spirits at Xango Cá Te Espero: Babá Ọ̀lọ́jadé whom I discuss in subsequent chapters.

42. *Xango* is the Portuguese spelling of Ṣàngó, the Yorùbá thunder deity.

Chapter 2: Diary 1 2006: "She Is Standing Right Behind You"

1. See Thompson's seminal work on African altars, *Face of the Gods: Art and Altars of Africa and the African Americas* (New York: Museum for African Art, 1993). Also see Thompson, *Flash of the Spirit: African and Afro-American Art and Philosophy* (New York: Vintage Books, 1983), and his many other publications on the Afro-Atlantic artistic and religious traditions.

2. The formal name of the terreiro, literally House of Axé (spiritual power) of Aganjú (the Òrìṣà of the volcano).

3. Sadly, Zenaide passed away in 2010, *ibae* (rest in peace).

4. A terreiro is often surrounded by a high concrete wall, containing separate small rooms or individual houses for each Òrìṣà; a barracão, a large room for events; and a separate smaller building for the veneration of the dead, necessarily an appropriate distance from the living quarters. Some members of the terreiro may live there full time, though this is not the case at Xango Cá Te Espero. The terreiro is a self-sufficient, communal entity—a microcosm of the world, if you will.

5. In this instance the obrigação was the ceremony of completion for an initiate of seven years. An *obrigação*—obligation—in this sense means a ceremony and/or an offering; the literal translation of "obligation" does not adequately cover its full meaning, though it is an obligation, a responsibility, and commitment to follow through with this ritual.

6. Pai Balbino is a very famous pae-de-santo (father of the saint) in Brazil. *Obaràyí* by Mariano (2009) tells his life story.

7. There was no psychotropic quality, it just affected me in that particular way.

8. At this time—mid-1980s in New York City—few people (if any) had any formal knowledge of Egúngún.

9. Shango is the anglicized spelling of Ṣàngó [Y], Xango [P]. The literal meaning of Ṣàngó Fúnkẹ́ is *Ṣàngó is given to me to take care of, or cherish.*

10. Betty also broke with Santería/Lukumí tradition by initiating to a second Òrìṣà in Africa, Babàlúaíyé. She introduced the idea of receiving a single tutelary Òrìṣà by initiating one of her godchildren in Brooklyn with only the "head" Òrìṣà, under the guidance of a Yorùbá babaláwo, not including the "four pillars" of the Cuban tradition. This practice was known as "head and foot." See Brown, *Santería Enthroned*, 134–38, for an in-depth discussion.

11. This was confirmed by one of Betty's goddaughters and also her son Ladé.

12. Ifágbèmí Àjànàkú was a main source of information and friendship for Thompson also.

13. Betty Barney, personal communication, 1986.

14. *Igbodú* means "sacred room" in Cuba; see Brown, *Santería Enthroned*, 117.

15. Santería/Lukumí was commonly referred to as "The Religion."

16. *Adjubona* (Oyúbona) means "second godmother of the initiation; assistant to the Iyalocha; cares for the Iyawó at all times." See Lydia Cabrera, *Anagó: Vocabulario Lucumí: El Yoruba Que Se Habla En Cuba* (La Habana: Ed. C.R., 1957), 293 (translation, Ivor Miller).

17. Ca. 1977.

18. *Ọ̀sá méjì*: méjì means twice, thus the original signal of Ọ̀sá indicated by nine open-mouth positions of the cowrie shells had fallen twice. This indicates one of the major odùs. Ọ̀sá is the odù or divinatory signal where Ọya, the mother of Egúngún, speaks.

19. Égun, Égum (P), and Egúngún are often used interchangeably, Égun sometimes substituting as an abbreviated version of Egúngún, or signifying a single or particular spirit, or as a generic term for spirit; *espírito* (P) or *muerto* (SP). This high tone mark of the first syllable follows Dos Santos (1969) and Abraham (1958); it is also the common diasporic pronunciation.

20. The àràbà, a highly respected personage (and my spiritual grandfather), was also an important friend and informant to Robert Thompson and Judith Gleason.

21. The first two African American initiates, Walter King and Christopher Oliana, were initiated in August 1959 into the *rama* (lineage within an ocha house) of Fermina Gómez in Matanzas, Cuba. See Brown, *Santería Enthroned*, 276–86.

22. She was "tired of being spoon-fed information by the Cubans." Personal communication Betty Barney, ca. 1984. Betty was far ahead of the curve in terms of interest in the Yorùbá roots of Santería.

23. The dilogun (consecrated cowrie shells) of one's Òrìṣà was essential to reconstituting the Òrìṣà upon arrival in the United States.

24. *Ifáladé*: "Ifá is the crown" (shortened to Ladé in common usage).

Chapter 3: Diary 2 2007: "I Miss You Already"

1. I also understand what it means to be a "horse" for Òrìṣà, in my case, Ọbàtálá. Horse is a common term for a medium of the Òrìṣà (as with the *loa* of Vodou). See Maya Deren, *Divine Horsemen: The Voodoo Gods of Haiti* (New York: Vanguard Press, 1953).

2. Mother of the saint, the title of an initiated priestess.

3. For more information on Ọya, see Judith Gleason, *Ọya: In Praise of an African Goddess* (San Francisco: HarperCollins, 1987).

4. Barracão: literally, "barracks." Has many interesting close cognates: it referred to the slave pens on coastal Africa and the Caribbean (*barracón* ([SP]); the book *Barracoon*, by Zora Heale Huston, describes them as "the structures used to detain Africans. . . . as simple as a 'slave shed' to a 'slave castle' wherein Africans were forced into cells of dungeons beneath the upper quarters of European administrators." Intentional or not, the open-doored structure now resonates with love and multiple levels of spiritual freedom. Zora Heale Huston, *Barracoon* (New York: Amistad/HarperCollins, 2018).

5. Personal communication with Babá Carlos, 2017. *Axé* [P] or *aṣe* [Y] means spiritual power, or the power to make things happen. Ifatokun Adejola informed me of the term *camieira* and *ọpá ọrun*, staff of heaven, personal communication 2021. It is also referred to as the staff of Oranmi-yan, "a reference to the ancient pole at the center of the world in Africa." See Murphy, *Working the Spirit*, 68.

6. I believe there is a unique concentration of aṣe achieved in Brazil within the terreiros, where a whole township is essentially reproduced microcosmically within the walls of the terreiro. Whereas in Yorùbáland Égun would roam the streets and surrounding area, all activity here takes place within the walled boundaries.

7. In this case *axé* (P), *aṣe* (Y) is used like an exclamatory punctuation. As in, "Amen, brother!" An exclamation of thanks and acknowledgment.

8. Babá Ọ̀lójadé, the king of spirits at Xango Cá Te Espero.

9. Babá Ọ̀lójadé is commonly referred to by members of the terreiro as "my king." I discuss this notion of kingship and Egúngún as it relates to Brazil and Yorùbáland in a subsequent chapter.

10. Known as *atǫkùn* or *amúìṣan* in Yorùbáland.

11. Gèlèdè is the exclusively female society of the Yorùbá, a female counterpart to Egúngún. See Henry John Drewal and Margaret Thompson Drewal, *Gèlèdè: Art and Female Power among the Yorùbá* (Bloomington: Indiana University Press, 1990); and Babatunde Lawal, *The Gèlèdè Spectacle: Art, Gender, and Social Harmony in an African Culture* (Seattle: University of Washington Press, 1996).

12. In this sense, *axé*, which has multiple meanings and inferences, means "spiritual power or knowledge."

13. Ebó is a purification made through offerings as indicated by an Òrìṣà or Ifá, but is also used in a generic sense to define personal rituals.

14. Verger was also initiated as a babaláwo. There is an excellent video about his life: *Pierre Verger: Mensageiro Entre Dois Mundos* (Messenger Between Two Worlds), directed by Lula Buarque de Hollanda (DVD, Paris: Europa Filmes, 1996).

15. I was to realize later that the festival in honor for Babá Ọlọjadé was one of several annual festivals honoring particular Egúns.

16. Adetunde was the name I received when I was initiated as a babaláwo. Adetunde means "the crown has returned."

17. Personal communication with Salim Washington, December 2019. When I discussed this idea with Salim (having heard him present this previously at one of his Coltrane lectures), he agreed wholeheartedly: "Yes, it's the same. You are exactly right."

18. Voeks, *Sacred Leaves of Candomblé*, 67–68.

19. *Orixa funfun* (Y) means the collective group of *funfun* (white) Òrìṣà. *White* signifies an immaculateness of character and, as Thompson reveals: "the ultimate purity, the hope for transparent honesty" represented by the white clothes of the wearer. It is not in any way an allusion to race. See Thompson, lecture on *The Daughters of the Dust*, 2006. Accessed April 18, 2020, https://www.youtube.com/watch?v=b3oHa Ci5fq4. See also William Bascomb, *Ifá Divination: Communication between Gods and Men in West Africa* (Bloomington: Indiana University Press, 1969), 103, 185, n3.

Chapter 4: Diary 3 2008–2012: Obrigação

1. *Iaô* (P) refers to a new initiate. From the Yorùbá ìyàwó, wife.

2. *abô* is a bath of sacred herbs, essential to any initiation process. Virtually every initiation I am familiar with in African diaspora traditions includes cleansing baths of consecrated herbs; it is an obligatory element.

3. Èṣù is the Òrìṣà of all paths and possibilities, the deity that makes possible the delivery of messages and offerings to Olódùmarè. No ritual can commence without consulting and acknowledging Èṣù first.

4. *Obì kọla* (*cola acuminata*) common to Brazil is the two-segmented variety known in Africa as *obì gbanja* (Y). In Africa, it is the four-segmented variety, *obì àbàtà* (Y), that is used for divination. In Brazil, in order to produce the four necessary lobes, the *obì gbanja* is separated and then cut in half. Obì was imported since mid-nineteenth century and was successfully introduced to Brazilian soil: "Seeds were undoubtedly planted during the latter part of the nineteenth century." It was "purposely introduced from Africa and naturalized for its use in Candomblé ceremonies." Voeks, *Sacred Leaves of Candomblé*, 26–27, 45, 140.

5. A note on the drummers. Every young man in the terreiro plays drums and with great skill: they are virtuosic musicians. Every Amuxian and Ojé plays drums. They constantly take turns. Everyone knows the songs; participation in the common liturgy is effortless and second nature. Any member of the terreiro can start a song, male or female, though, for certain ritual moments a precise order is followed—these were led by Babá Carlos and his closest assistants.

6. *Equedi* means "second person," a female priestess who does not enter into trance of the Òrìṣà; because of this she is able to attend to the Òrìṣà and the mediums. In this event, Lenira also represented me as a godmother with Egúngún.

7. Babá Carlos Ojé Dúdú, personal communication.

8. "Mounted" is the term used throughout African diasporic religious traditions to describe the experience of an Òrìṣà possessing one's body.

9. "The breeze of blessing": see Maryanne Fitzgerald, Henry Drewal, and Moyo Ekedji, "Transformation Through Cloth: An Egúngún Costume of the Yorùbá," *African Arts* 28, no. 2 (Spring 1995): 56, 57.

10. Dos Santos, *Ancestor Worship*, 93.

11. In Calabar, Nigeria, author B. E. Bassey has described similar experiential transformations through Ékpe "leopard" society initiations. See Bassey Efiong Bassey, *Ékpè Efik: A Theosophical Perspective* (Victoria, BC: Trafford Publishing, 1998/2001), 11.

12. The òpèlè is a chain with four seed pods on each side—one of the tools of the Ifá diviner—which, when manipulated, will reveal one of 256 proverbial stories to guide a client's life.

13. The story Afro-Reggae is documented in the wonderful film *Favela Rising*, which outlines the circumstances and life events of its founder, Junior, that led to the birth of Afro-Reggae. See *Favela Rising*, directed by Jeff Zimbalist and Matt Mochary (DVD, Brazil: Side Track Films, 2005). See http://www.favelarising.com.

14. My career situation was resolved positively in my favor; my dismissal was reversed, and I retired the following October.

Chapter 5: Diary 4 2013: Amuxian

1. Robert Farris Thompson, *African Art in Motion* (Los Angeles: University of California Press, 1974), 219.

2. Dos Santos, *Ancestor Worship*, 96–97. Similarly, in southeast Nigeria, one must be summoned by *Ndem* to join *Ndem* "spirit" society, meaning *it's the most exclusive club around.* Ivor Miller, personal communication (2018).

3. In a statement professing and protecting the sanctity of the Egúngún cult, the president of the association states: "By having periodic meetings, the association maintains control of the Egúngún cult in Brazil, preserving those rites, as well as the records of new Amuxian and Ojé initiations in existing houses." Balbino Daniel de Paula, Facebook post (accessed 2018).

4. Omari-Tunkara, *Manipulating the Sacred*, 94.

5. Dos Santos, *Ancestor Worship*, 96–97.

6. Dos Santos, *Ancestor Worship*, 106–7.

7. See, for example, José Jorge de Carvalho and Rita Segato, *Shango Cult in Recife, Brazil* (Caracas, Venezuela: FUNDEF, 1992); Roger Bastide, *The African Religions of Brazil: Toward a Sociology of the Interpenetration of Civilizations*, trans. by H. Sebba (Baltimore: Johns Hopkins University Press, [1960] 2007).

8. The only strict time requirement was the start of ceremonies at 7 a.m. on Saturday morning!

9. In the Lukumí system, you receive the title of Oluwo if you have been initiated into Òrìṣà and also Ifá. I have this, but I am also Oluwo because of the title given to me by Egúngún.

10. *Orí* means "inner consciousness" in Yorùbá.

11. Vows of secrecy are inherent in other religions and spiritual practices; all contain their own deeply secretive inner circles of knowledge. I advocate that even that which is not secret per se, should not be viewed in a casual manner, without effort. Sacred moments and rituals should best be preserved, viewed, and experienced from within the confines of practice, not viewed voyeuristically outside of an experiential context.

12. While Babá Carlos is the godfather to all of us in the terreiro, other intermediate godfathers and godmothers stand with and represent initiates through different ceremonies.

13. The family structure here is gone into in detail in Carvalho and Segato, *Shango Cult.*

14. Thompson, personal communication, January 2017. *Igbala* means "something that saves a person," referring to the saw-toothed borders on the cloth panels of certain Egúngún. See Thompson, *African Art in Motion*, 219.

15. In the days that followed, while discussing a part of the ceremony with Ojé Dúdú and my brothers, I remarked that I did not remember that part at all. Everyone was surprised—me especially so. Ojé Dúdú just smiled and said: "Even better. Ọbàtálá." In this sense he was stating that Ọbàtálá as my Òrìṣà had come so close to me that I was no longer very aware of events.

16. I believe those readers who were fortunate enough to know Betty would smile at this portrayal, remembering her spirit.

17. Ìyàmi Òṣòròngà means, literally, "our mothers," who represent repositories of the deepest female energy. In common use they are erroneously labeled as "witches."

Chapter 6: Diary 5 2016:
Visiting the Matrix: A Trip to Itaparica

1. "A kind of clay we call *tupitinga*, white in color," personal communication with Ailton Benedito de Sousa, resident of Itaparica, 2019.

2. There is a wonderful quote by Goethe: "At the moment of decision the universe conspires to assist you."

3. Ògún is the Òrìṣà of war, iron, and the forest.

4. Sacred to both Africa and Brazil, the ìrokò tree in Brazil is the residence of the Òrìṣà Ìrokò, the god of time.

5. Cornelius O. Adepegba, "Intriguing Aspects of Yorùbá Masquerade," *Nigerian Field* 55 (April 1990): 4.

6. Fitzgerald, et al., "Transformation Through Cloth," 55.

7. Betty Barney (Ṣàngó Funké), personal communication.

8. Eliseu Martiniano do Bonfim (the last Brazilian babaláwo) and Mãe Aninha (Eugenia Ana dos Santos) proudly recreated the institution of the twelve paths (or *obás*—ministers of Xango) at Ilê Axé Opô Afonjá. See Stefania Capone, *Searching for Africa in Brazil: Power and Tradition in Candomblé* (Durham, NC: Duke University Press, 2010), 223, 225. Also see J. Lorand Matory, *Black Atlantic Religion: Tradition, Transnationalism, and Matriarchy in the Afro-Brazilian Candomblé* (Princeton, NJ: Princeton University Press, 2005), 129–48, for an in-depth examination of the idea of "African purity" within houses of Candomblé.

9. The tradition of the *Mesa Blanca* (white table) séances of Kardecian spiritualism, a deep and profound practice, was an essential method

for diasporic followers of Òrìṣà to maintain contact with the dead. Mesa blanca was my first, and in some ways most important, training in spiritual and occult studies—that of the *espiritiste*—a full possession medium who works the spirits of the dead.

Part II: Egúngún: Custodians of Endless Memory

1. Thompson, *African Art in Motion*, 219.

Chapter 7: Ancient Kings Emerge

1. Ifáyẹmí Elẹ́buibọn, *The Healing Power of Sacrifice* (New York: Athelia Henrietta Press, 2000), 134. This evocative and poignant poetic statement assures those left behind of continued communication with their loved ones, through visions, dreams, and Ifá divination.

2. Dos Santos, *Ancestor Worship*, 85.

3. Personal communication with Baba Carlos, April 2016.

4. Personal communication, 2019. Adewale simplified the term even further by eliminating the "male" qualifier.

5. Babayemi, *Egúngún among the Ọ̀yọ́ Yorùbá*, 3.

6. Ivor Miller, personal communication, 2019. "Some may consider the reference to Egúngún as Ancient Kings as a romanticized appellation." Dr. Miller points out that the idea of Egúngún being kings was not common in Yorùbáland. He suggests that throughout the Americas, the notion of kingship "has been a poetic method of confronting the inhumanity of slavery by raising the status of the individual."

7. Pierre Verger, "The Rise and Fall of the Worship of Ìyàmi Òṣòròngà among the Yorùbá," in *Pierre Fatumbi Verger Articles, Vol. I*, translated by Christophe Brunski (New Jersey: Black Madonna Enterprises, [1965] 2007), 62.

8. Omari-Tunkara, *Manipulating the Sacred*, 56, back cover. (In Ilé Obaerin in Pernambuco, Recife, the logo of the temple is a gold crown.)

9. Lawal confirms this as true in Africa also: ". . . *the word of the ancestors is law.*" Babatunde Lawal, "The Living Dead: Art and Immortality among the Yorùbá of Nigeria," *Africa: Journal of the International African Institute* 47, no. 1 (1977): 59.

10. A person's patron Òrìṣà is normally revealed through a reading of buzios [cowrie shells] or Ifá divination.

11. Dos Santos, *Ancestor Worship*, 83. "Égun Olúkọ̀tún is considered one of the ancestors of the true Yorùbá race." Also see Mariano, *Obaràyí*,

587, n6. Olúkộtún is also a proper name, belonging to a founding ancestor of a lineage of Éguns in Yorùbáland.

12. P. S. O. Aremu, "The Figures of Power: Reflections upon Power
and Identity in the Yorùbá Egúngún Worship," *Nigerian Heritage* 7
(1998): 66.

13. Mariano, *Obaràyí*, 587, n4.

14. Dos Santos, *Ancestor Worship*, 79.

15. A Catholic church in Drogheda, Republic of Ireland, famously
has a complete head of their patron saint, Oliver Plunkett, a seven-
teenth-century Irish martyr, along with glass display cases of his individual bones. When I walked into the church—and was greeted at eye
level by the head of Saint Plunkett—I thought: "This poor guy will never
rest." Early churches all over the Christian world have bones of priests as
sacred items.

16. P. S. O. Aremu, "Spiritual and Physical Identity of Yorùbá Egúngún
Costumes: A General Survey," *Nigeria Magazine* 47 (1983): 47.

17. Aremu calls them *"ará ộrun kinkin, the immaculate from
heaven."* Aremu, "Figures of Power," 62.

18. Dos Santos, *Ancestor Worship*, 85.

19. Dos Santos, *Ancestor Worship*, 87. See also Henry Drewal and
Margaret Drewal, *Gệlệdệ: Art and Female Power among the Yorùbá*
(Bloomington: Indiana University Press), 1990.

20. Babatunde Lawal, *The Gệlệdệ Spectacle: Art, Gender, and Social
Harmony in an African Culture* (Seattle: University of Washington
Press, 1996), xiv, 262.

21. Margaret Drewal, *Yorùbá Ritual: Performers, Play, Agency*
(Bloomington: Indiana University Press, 1992), 202.

22. See Verger, *Ìyàmi Òṣòròngà*, 59–61. See also Babayemi, *Egúngún
among the Ộyộ Yorùbá*, 11, 13.

23. Verger, *Ìyàmi Òṣòròngà*, 59–61.

24. According to Babayemi, e.g., in Ègbádò the female title holders
are *Ìyá Agan, Otun Ìyá Agan*, and *Iyamako*. Babayemi, *Egúngún among
the Ộyộ Yorùbá*, 5.

25. Gleason, *Ọya*, 6.

26. Dos Santos, *Ancestor Worship*, 79 n1. See also Voeks, *Sacred
Leaves of Candomblé*, 61–63, for an insightful discussion of the Candomblé concept of heaven. For additional concepts of heaven and
post-mortem judgment, see J. Omosade Awolalu, *Yorùbá Beliefs and
Sacrificial Rites* (New York: Athelia Henrietta Press, 1979), 58–59.

27. Ajuwon, "Ògún's Ìrèmòjé," 194.

28. E. Bólájí Ìdòwú, *Olódùmarè: God in Yorùbá Belief* (New York:
Wazobia, 1962), 189.

29. Babayemi, *Egúngún among the Ọ̀yọ́ Yorùbá*, 18–21. Babayemi discusses both possible origins.

30. Peter Morton-Williams, "Yorùbá Responses to the Fear of Death," *Africa: Journal of the International African Institute* 30, no. 1 (January 1960): 36.

31. Lawal, "The Living Dead," 59.

32. Cleidiana Ramos, "The Cult of the Egun Preserves the Collective Bond," *A Tarde* (2014). Accessed February 2018. http://atarde.uol.com.br/muito/noticias/1635733-balbino-o-culto-a-Egúngún-preserva-o-laco-coletivo.

33. Thompson, *African Art in Motion*, 219.

Chapter 8: Origins of Egúngún

1. Karin Barber, *I Could Speak until Tomorrow: Oríkì, Women and the Past in a Yorùbá Town* (Washington DC: Smithsonian Institution Press, 1991), 76.

2. J. A. Adedeji, "The Origin of the Yorùbá Masque Theatre: The Use of Ifá Divination Corpus as Historical Evidence," *African Notes* 6, no. 1 (1970): 80.

3. Babayemi, *Egúngún*, 10.

4. Thompson, *African Arts*, 219, relates: Ṣàngó was saved from illness as "his followers used part of the Egúngún dress, the panels with the sawtooth border, known as *igbala* (something that saves a person)."

5. Adedeji, "The Origin of the Yorùbá Masque Theatre: The Use of Ifá Divination," 80. See also Robert Smith, "The Alafin in Exile: A Study of the Igboho Period in Ọ̀yọ́ History," *Journal of African History* 6, no. 1 (1965): 59.

6. Smith, "The Alafin in Exile," 65. See also Adedeji, "The Origin and Form of the Yorùbá Masque Theatre," *Cahiers d'études Africaines* 12, no. 46 (1972): 255, for further information on Ọ̀yọ́ and Egúngún.

7. Aremu, "Spiritual and Physical Identity," 63.

8. E. Bọ́laji Ìdòwú, *African Traditional Religion: A Definition* (Maryknoll, NY: Orbis Books, 1973), 188.

9. The 1978 *African Arts* issue dedicated solely to Egúngún reports a wide variety of descriptions and classifications of Egúngún in different territories. See Henry and Margaret Thompson Drewal, "More Powerful Than Each Other: An Ẹ̀gbádò Classification of Egúngún," *African Arts* 11, no. 3 (April 1978): 28–39, 99.

10. Personal communication with Baba Carlos, 2019. Baba Carlos referenced this as the "holy trinity."

11. Ramos, "The Cult of the Egun."

12. Mariano, *Obaráyí*, 588n10.

13. Ilê Axé Opô Afonjá is the original terreiro of Babá Carlos's family. Babá Carlos's godfather was the godbrother of the late Mae Estella. Personal communication with Cintia Burgues da Rocha, 2021.

14. Zen Buddhism speaks of "waiting for the flashing." See Shunryo Suzuki, *Zen Mind, Beginner's Mind* (New York: Weatherhill, 1995), 82.

15. Thompson's translation of *Xango Cá Té Espero*.

16. Thompson, personal communication, 2012.

Chapter 9: Change and Continuity: From Africa to Brazil

1. Henry Drewal, "Whirling Cloth, Breeze of Blessing: Egúngún Masquerades among the Yorùbá," in *Homecomings, Crossings, and Passings: Life and Death in the African Diaspora*, edited by Regennia N. Williams (Porter Ranch, CA: New World African Press, 2011), 185.

2. Both the colobus (*ẹdun* [Y]) and the red savannah patas guenon monkey (ìjímèrè [Y]) are referenced in Africa. The monkey is central to many of the Egúngún creation myths. Margaret Thompson Drewal, *Yorùbá Ritual: Performers, Play, Agency* (Bloomington: Indiana University Press, 1992), 93–94. See also Babayemi, *Egúngún among the Ọ̀yọ́ Yorùbá*, 6–9, 15.

3. "high-pitched, quavering voice": John Pemberton, "Egúngún Masquerades of the Igbomina People," *African Arts* 11, no. 3 (April 1978): 41.

4. *eegi* [P], *ṣẹ́gi* [Y].

5. Adewale, personal communication, 2019: titles include Ìyá Agan, the highest title. Gleason, *Ọya*, 306: *ato*, assigned to female triplets. Abímbọ́lá, *Bag of Wisdom*, 153, states that this name is also given to female children born holding their umbilical cord; if male he is called amúisàn.

6. For more information on the *Gẹ̀lẹ̀dẹ̀*, see Drewal and Drewal, *Gẹ̀lẹ̀dẹ̀*; and Lawal, *The Gẹ̀lẹ̀dẹ̀ Spectacle*.

7. In Brazil these whips are made from the biribá tree (*rollinia deliciosa*). Interestingly, this is also the tree used to make the berimbau. Stela Guedes Caputo, Accessed June 1, 2018. https://www.scribd.com/document/74342578/entrevista-sobre-Egúngún.

8. Egúngún can also carry the ìṣan: Verger, *Ewe*, 28–29, quoted in Marilyn Houlberg Hammersley, "Notes on Egúngún Masquerades among the Ọ̀yọ́ Yorùbá," *African Arts* 11, no. 3 (April 1978): 61, states "the àtòrì is the wood used for ìṣan, it is traditionally for calm in the house, and cites an Osogbo babaláwo: *Eegun ki ijade ko ma mu ore l'owo. (The ghost does not go out without the whip in his hands.)*"

9. Èmi lọmọ arí ṣan kan pe ìgba Eégún jọ: "With one Àtòrì whip I invite two hundred Egúngún." From an Oríkì Ìgbórì (praise poetry

from Ìgbórì, a town in Nigeria), in Babayemi, *Egúngún among the Ọ̀yọ́ Yorùbá*, 66–67.

10. This cautioning is enforced very strictly in Brazil. You may see pictures of people casually touching or hugging Egúngún on the internet; this does not happen in Brazil.

11. Omari, *Manipulating the Sacred*, 92.

12. Ìdòwú, *Olódùmarè*, 192.

13. Bascomb (1969, 93) in Oludare Olajubu and J. R. O. Ojo, "Some Aspects of Ọ̀yọ́ Yorùbá Masquerades," *Africa: Journal of the International African Institute* 47, no. 3 (1977): 255: "According to an Inisha informant, when the world was created in Ifẹ (regarded by the Yorùbá as the center of the world), the secrets (awo) of *Egúngún*; *ishegun* (compounding of medicine); and Ifá divination, were born in that order of seniority."

14. Liner notes for *Egúngún, Ancestralidade Africana no Brasil* (LP, SECNEB-Brazilian Society for Black Culture Studies, 1982), one of the first records of the *lesé* Egun cult of Itaparica.

15. *Egúngún Ancestralidade Africana no Brasil,* liner notes.

16. Personal communication with Henry Drewal, December 2019.

17. Personal communication with Babá Carlos, April 2016.

18. Balbino Daniel de Paula, comment on Facebook, accessed July 2019, rebuking a man claiming to be an Ọ̀jẹ̀ for which there is no record.

19. Adewale Bógunmbẹ̀, personal communication, 2019.

20. Interestingly, Martiniano—who as regarded as an expert in Yorùbá traditional religion—was an Ọ̀jẹ̀, his initiatory name was Ojeladê. Mariano, *Obaràyí*, 597. Martiniano's father was also an Ọ̀jẹ̀ (personal communication with Lisa Earl Castillo, 2019). There is a fascinating book by Ruth Landes, *City of Women* (Albuquerque: University of New Mexico Press, 1947); the author speaks a great deal about Martiniano, and gives the reader a unique sense of that time period in Bahia.

21. There is a resurgence of Ifá in Brazil brought about by both Cuban and African babaláwos emigrating there.

22. Omari-Tunkara, *Manipulating the Sacred*, 94.

23. An Ọ̀jẹ̀ does not go through the aparaká stage.

24. Personal communication with Babá Carlos, 2015.

25. When the bodily form is not recognizable, the Egúngún represents some abstract aspect related to death. Dos Santos, *Ancestor Worship*, 86.

26. Dana Rush, *Vodun in Coastal Bénin: Unfinished, Open-Ended, Global* (Nashville, TN: Vanderbilt University Press, 2013), 68.

27. Karin Barber, *I Could Speak until Tomorrow: Oríkì, Women, and the Past in a Yorùbá Town* (Washington DC: Smithsonian Institution Press, 1991), 313.

28. Adewale Bógunmbẹ̀, personal communication, 2019.

29. Marilyn Hammersley Houlberg, "Egúngún Masquerades of the Remo Yorùbá," *African Arts* 11, no. 3 (April 1978a): 20, 25–26.

30. Thompson, *African Art in Motion*, 221–22.

31. Norma H. Wolff, "Egúngún Costuming in Abeokuta," *African Arts* 15, no. 3 (May 1982): 66.

32. My observations about Brazilian Egúngún are based on what I witnessed during numerous visits to Xango Cá Te Espero, interviews, and published research.

33. Aremu, "Figures of Power," 63.

34. Brandon, *Santeria from Africa to the New World*," 15.

35. See Adedeji, "The Origin of the Yorùbá Masque Theatre," 70, 72–73.

36. Babayemi, *Egúngún of Ọ̀yọ́*, 10. (This is just one of many Egúngún origin stories.)

Chapter 10: A Mysterious Wind: Aparaká

1. Babá Carlos, personal communication, April 2016.

2. Thompson, personal communication, January 2017.

3. James Wafer, *The Taste of Blood: Spirit Possession in Brazilian Candomblé* (Austin: University of Texas Press, 1997), 185–86. The author's firsthand account. This celebration took place in Bahia.

4. Marc Schiltz, "Egúngún Masquerades in Iganna," *African Arts* 11, no. 3 (1978): 52.

5. John Pemberton, "Egúngún Masquerades of the Igbomina People," *African Arts* 11, no. 3 (April 1978): 41–42.

6. Henry Drewal, "The Arts of Egúngún among the Yorùbá Peoples," *African Arts* 11, no. 3 (April 1978): 18.

7. Wande Abímbọ́lá, *Ifá: An Exposition of Ifá Literary Corpus* (New York: Athelia Henrietta Press, 1997), 249.

8. Thompson, *Face of the Gods*, 197.

9. Barber's phrase describes a locus of in-between-ness I have referred to previously as the abode of Egúngún and other spiritual beings or, perhaps more accurately, the portal or the meeting ground between heaven and earth, where the invisible inhabitants may be accessed by humans, in this particular case an exhortation of Ṣàngó. Barber, *I Could Speak until Tomorrow*, 77.

10. *ixan* (P), *işan* [Y]: a spiritually charged whip—a slender branch—used to invoke Egúngún by the Ọ̀jẹ̀s, and to protect and separate the Babá Éguns from the people, holding them back by pressing against their gown with the *ixan*. The attendants of Egúngún, the Amuxian (also known as *atọ̀kùn* or *amúìşan* in Yorùbáland), bearers of the ìxan, have this duty. The ixan is made from the biriba tree (*rollinia deliciosa*) in Brazil; in Yorùbáland it is made from the àtòrì tree (*glyphaea lateriflora* [a tree that brings calm]). Verger, *Ewé*, 664.

11. Dos Santos, *Ancestor Worship*, 86.

12. Thompson, personal communication, 2015.

13. Lawal, "The Living Dead," 59.

14. Rowland Abiodun, "Hidden Power: Ọ̀ṣun, the Seventeenth Odù," in Murphy and Sanford, *Ọ̀ṣun Across the Waters*, 24.

15. A woman is not allowed to enter the shrine of Egúngún unless she was born with the umbilical cord in her hand. Such female children are called *ato*, and (in Yorùbáland) they are allowed to know all the secrets of Egúngún. Wande Abímbọ́lá, "The Bag of Wisdom: Ọ̀ṣun and the Origins of Ifá Divination," in Murphy and Sanford, *Ọ̀ṣun Across the Waters*, 153.

16. Thompson, personal communication, 2012.

17. Thompson, personal communication, 2015.

18. Thompson, personal communication, 2012.

19. Thompson, personal communication, June 2017.

20. Ivor Miller references an alternative to "masquerade" from the Abakuá society: "The body mask of the Ékpe and Abakuá Íreme represents the presence of the ancestors of the group." See Lydia Cabrera, *The Sacred Language of the Abakuá*, trans. Ivor Miller and P. González (Jackson: University Press of Mississippi, 2020), xi, xxix, 8.

21. In conversation with Henry Drewal, 2019.

22. Adedeji, "The Origin of the Yorùbá Masque Theatre," 76n16.

23. Mikelle Smith Omari, "The Role of the Gods in Afro-Brazilian Ancestral Ritual," *African Arts* 23, no. 1 (1989): 103n4.

24. Ìdòwú, *Olódùmarè*, 190.

25. Thompson, *African Art in Motion*, 225.

26. P. S. O. Aremu, "Between Myth and Reality: Yorùbá Egúngún Costumes as Commemorative Clothes," *Journal of Black Studies* 22, no. 1 (Sept. 1991): 9.

27. Aremu, "Between Myth and Reality," 7.

28. Caputo, "To Weave the Sacred Opá."

29. Thompson, personal communication, 2015.

30. Norma H. Wolff, "Egúngún Costuming in Abeokuta," *African Arts* 15, no. 3 (May 1982): 66–67.

31. Wolff, "Egúngún Costuming in Abeokuta," 67.

32. Caputo, "To Weave the Sacred Opá." In this enlightening article, Caputo portrays one such spiritual apprenticeship.

Chapter 11: Mother of Nine

1. Judith Gleason, *Ọya*, 9. This praise poem was collected by Fela Sowande and Ifágbèmí Àjànàkú in the 1960s.

2. Mariano, *Obaràyí*, 657.

3. Gleason, *Ọya*, 1–2. See chapter 11.

4. This role as "resolver-of-disputes" was inherited by her child—Egúngún. For a more in-depth discussion on Ọya, see Gleason, *Ọya*.

5. Gleason, *Ọya*, 1.

6. Roy C. Abraham, *Dictionary of Modern Yorùbá* (London: University of London Press, 1958), 293. Both the ìjímèrè, patas monkey (*erythrocebus patas*), and the ẹdun, colobus monkey (*colobus angolensis*), are associated with Egúngún. According to Babayemi, *Egúngún among the Ọ̀yọ́ Yorùbá*, 9n1, there is no difference in the description of ìjímèrè and ẹdun in the context of Egúngún oríkì or Ifá odù.

7. A single termite queen can lay thousands of eggs in a day, hence the efficacy of the termite mound as a fertility charm.

8. Thompson, *Face of the Gods*, 193. Countless references view the *patas* monkey and its manner of speech as similar to that of Egúngún; the monkey is representative of Egúngún on multiple levels, as well as being "central to myths about the origin of Egúngún"; M. Drewal, *Yorùbá* Ritual, 94. Gleason describes "a true totemic affiliation between Egúngún and that almost-human primate"; Gleason, *Ọya*, 100.

9. Voeks, *Sacred Leaves of Candomblé*, 63.

10. Thompson, personal communication, January 2015.

11. Abímbọ́lá and Miller, *Ifá Will Mend*, 157–58.

12. "Yansan 'Bale, rules cemeteries and *the dead*" (italics mine); Omari-Tunkara, *Manipulating the Sacred*, 149.

13. "*Ira*—Rome, or Mecca to the Ọya-worshipper"; Gleason, *Ọya*, 12.

14. Interview with Babá Carlos, Ojé Dúdú, April 2016.

Chapter 12: Timeline: A Miracle of Memory and Perseverance

1. Eltis and Richardson, *Atlas of the Transatlantic Slave Trade*, 203, 303.

2. Eltis and Richardson, *Atlas of the Transatlantic Slave Trade*, 203. Also see Eltis, "Diaspora of Yorùbá Speakers," 28.

3. The "Slave Coast" was also known as the Bight of Bénin, a bay of the Atlantic Ocean on the coast of western Africa, which gave its name to a slaving region. The Bight of Bénin slaving region stretched about 400 miles along the coast, from Cape St. Paul east to the Nun River (an extension of the Niger). Today the coastline is part of eastern Ghana, Togo, Bénin, and western Nigeria. Eltis and Richardson, *Atlas of the Transatlantic Slave Trade*, 302.

4. Eltis, "The Diaspora of Yorùbá Speakers," 28. See also João José Reis and Beatriz Galotti Mamigonian, "Nago and Mina: The Yorùbá

Diaspora in Brazil," in *The Yorùbá Diaspora in the Atlantic World*, edited by Toyin Falola and Matt D. Childs (Bloomington: Indiana University Press, 2004), 77–78.

5. James Murphy, *Working the Spirit: Ceremonies of the African Diaspora* (Boston: Beacon Press, 1994), 47–48. Also see Reis and Mamigonian, "Nago and Mina," 80.

6. See Robin Law, "Ethnicity and the Slave Trade: 'Lucumí' and 'Nago' as Ethnonyms in West Africa," *History of Africa* 24 (1997): 212–15.

7. Dos Santos, *Ancestor Worship*, 79.

8. Murphy, *Working the Spirit*, 48–49.

9. Mariano, *Obaràyí*, 588.

10. Ailton Benedito Sousa, personal communication, 2019.

11. Omari-Tunkara, *Manipulating the Sacred*, 90–93.

12. J. Lorand Matory, *Black Atlantic Religion: Tradition, Transnationalism, and Matriarchy in the Afro-Brazilian Candomblé* (Princeton, NJ: Princeton University Press, 2005), 65.

13. For more information on this "second migration," see Solimar Otero, *Afro-Cuban Diasporas in the Atlantic World* (Rochester, NY: Boydell and Brewer, 2010); Falola and Childs, *The Yorùbá Diaspora*; and Kristen Mann and Edna G. Bay, eds., *Rethinking the African Diaspora: The Making of a Black Atlantic World in the Bight of Bénin and Brazil* (London: Frank Cass, 2001). See also Omari-Tunkara, *Manipulating the Sacred*, 92.

14. Robin Law, "The Evolution of the Brazilian Community in Ouidah," in Mann and Bay, *Rethinking the African Diaspora*, 26.

15. *assento*: literally, seat. This refers to the fundamental ritually prepared physical object in which a spirit would be "seated"; said object would house a particular spirit.

16. Pierre Verger, *Noticias da Bahia: 1850* (Salvador, Bahia), 229. "As many as ninety-one trips were documented for 1848": Omari-Tunkara, *Manipulating the Sacred*, 92.

17. http://issuu.com/adrianpsy/docs/926-1969-1-pb (15). This further evidences exchange taking place between Bahia and West Africa in the nineteenth century and onward, showing Egúngún so firmly established in Bahia that it could be exported back to its continent of origin. I speculate that this must have been a gift to honor the Bamgboshe household, Şàngó and Egúngún, all.

18. Mariano, *Obaràyí*; Dos Santos, *Os Nágôs e a Morte*.

19. Dos Santos, *Ancestor Worship*, 82.

20. Mariano, *Obaràyí*, 587. "According to the linguist Felix Ayoh'Omidere, Olúkòtún is also a proper name, belonging to a founding ancestor of a lineage of *Éguns* in Yorùbáland (the African region where the

Yorùbá culture dominates) that was later taken to Brazil." According to
Dos Santos, *Ancestor Worship in Bahia*, 83, *Égun Olúkòtún* was "considered one of the ancestors of the true *Yorùbá* race." And from Babá
Carlos: "*Olúkòtún*: he [lord] who sits at the right side of God," personal
communication, 2016.

21. Ponta da Areia—the village on the island of Itaparica—was an old
quilombo, fugitive slave community. Much of the Daniel de Paula family
still reside in the locality. Mariano, *Obaràyí*, 172.

22. Dos Santos notes: "Information concerning the founders of Encarnaçao is contradictory and confusing; the first chief about whom information is available is João Dois Metres." Dos Santos, *Ancestor Worship*,
83–84. This is confirmed by Mariano, *Obaràyí*, 663.

23. There is occasionally conflicting information: Dos Santos argues
that Babá Agboulá was invoked there for the first time in Brazil, but,
as mentioned above, Mariano quotes Tio Serafim's grandsons stating
that Agboulá was invoked already at Vera Cruz, and then brought to
Encarnação.

24. Mariano, *Obaràyí*, 587. "According to the linguist Felix Ayoh'Omidere, Agboulá is a proper name derived from the Yorùbá word
Agboolá." Olúkòtún is also a proper name, belonging to a founding
ancestor of a lineage of *Éguns* in Yorùbáland (the African region where
the Yorùbá culture dominates) that was later taken to Brazil.

25. Mariano, *Obaràyí*, 587–88.

26. *A Tarde*, June 21, 1940.

27. Mariano, *Obaràyí*, 589.

28. In my 2016 interview with Bàbá Carlos, he states: "Ilê Agboulá is
from the same year I was born, 1957."

29. Mariano, *Obaràyí*, 664.

30. Dos Santos, *Ancestor Worship*, 85.

31. Babá Carlos, personal communication, 2016.

32. The singular head of the entire Egúngún cult in Brazil.

33. Thompson told me of the existence of four remaining houses in
the 1980s; personal communication, 1985. Omari speaks of only two.
Omari-Tunkara, *Manipulating the Sacred*, 93.

34. Here again I propose that the isolation of the island may have
helped keep the family unit more intact and facilitated the familial adherence to and the organizational structure of the Egúngún cult.

35. Robert Farris Thompson, "The Three Warriors: Atlantic Altars of
Èṣù, Ògún, and Ọṣọosi," in *The Yorùbá Artist: New Theoretical Perspectives on African Arts*, edited by Rowland Abiodun, Henry J. Drewal, and
John Pemberton III (Washington, DC: Smithsonian Institution Press,
1994), 239.

Chapter 13: "And Then There Was the Letter"

1. A high-ranking post in a terreiro.
2. Obaluayê, also known as Omolu, is the patron divinity of smallpox, infectious disease, and leprosy. Asobá is a post or rank in worship of Obaluaiyê.
3. Special thanks to Lisa Earl Castillo for tracking down and confirming this name, personal communication, 2019.
4. Ajuwon, "Ògún's Ìrèmòjé," 195.

Chapter 14: Conclusion

1. Ìdòwú, African *Traditional Religion*, 188. African invocation to the ancestors, remembered and unremembered, known and unknown.
2. The Association includes my terreiro, listed as Babá Òlójadé, referring to the member terreiros by the name of their patron Babá Égun.
3. Peter Morton-Williams, "Yorùbá Responses to the Fear of Death," *Africa: Journal of the International African Institute* 30, no. 1 (January 1960): 39.
4. Cornelius O. Adepegba, "Intriguing Aspects of Yorùbá Masquerade," *Nigerian Field* 55 (April 1990): 3.
5. Abímbólá and Miller, *Ifá Will Mend*, 67.
6. "Nana" speaking to Eli, in Julie Dash's magnificent film *Daughters of the Dust* (1991).
7. From the Ifá Odù *Ogberíkúsá*. The story in this Odù reflects the political and social function of Egúngún, i.e., to rid the society of all forces of instability. Babayemi, *Egúngún among the Òyó Yorùbá*, 10.

Glossary

1. Ulli Beier, "The Egúngún Cult," *Nigeria Magazine* 51 (1956): 382.
2. Dos Santos, *Ancestor Worship*, 93.
3. Gleason, *Oya*, 78.
4. Dos Santos, *Ancestor Worship*, 83.
5. Dos Santos, *Ancestor Worship*, 108.
6. Ivor Miller, personal communication, 2019.

WORKS CITED

Abímbọlá, Wande, and Ivor Miller. *Ifá Will Mend This Broken World*. Roxbury, MA: Aim Books, 1997.

Abímbọlá, Wande. *Ifá: An Exposition of Ifá Literary Corpus*. New York: Athelia Henrietta Press, 1997.

Abiodun, Rowland, Henry J. Drewal, and John Pemberton III, eds. *The Yorùbá Artist: New Theoretical Perspectives on African Arts*. Washington, DC: Smithsonian Institution Press, 1994.

Abiodun, Rowland. "Hidden Power: Ọṣun, the Seventeenth Odù." In *Ọṣun Across the Waters*, eds. Joseph Murphy and Mei-Mei Sanford, 10–33. Bloomington: Indiana University Press, 2001.

Abraham, Roy C. *Dictionary of Modern Yorùbá*. London: University of London Press, 1958.

Adedeji, J. A. "The Origin and Form of the Yorùbá Masque Theatre." *Cahiers d'études Africaines* 12, no. 46 (1972): 254–76.

Adedeji, J. A. "The Origin of the Yorùbá Masque Theatre: The Use of Ifá Divination Corpus as Historical Evidence." *African Notes* 6, no. 1 (1970): 70–86.

Adepegba, Cornelius O. "Intriguing Aspects of Yorùbá Masquerade." *Nigerian Field* 55 (April 1990): 3–12.

Ajuwon, 'Bade. "Ògún's Ìrèmòjé: A Philosophy of Living and Dying." In *Africa's Ògún: Old World and New*, edited by Sandra Barnes, 173–98. Bloomington: Indiana University Press, 1997.

Aremu, P. S. O. "Between Myth and Reality: Yorùbá Egúngún Costumes as Commemorative Clothes." In *Journal of Black Studies* 22, no. 1 (Sept. 1991): 6–14.

Aremu, P. S. O. "The Figures of Power: Reflections upon Power and Identity in the Yorùbá Egúngún Worship." *Nigerian Heritage* 7 (1998): 62–73.

Aremu, P. S. O. "Spiritual and Physical Identity of Yorùbá Egúngún Costumes: A General Survey." *Nigeria Magazine* 47 (1983): 47–54.

Awolalu, J. Omosade. *Yorùbá Beliefs and Sacrificial Rites*. New York: Athelia Henrietta Press, 1979.

Babayemi, S. O. *Egúngún Among the Ọyọ Yorùbá*. Ibadan, Nigeria: Board Publications, 1980.

Barber, Karin. *I Could Speak until Tomorrow: Oríkì, Women and the Past in a Yorùbá Town*. Washington DC: Smithsonian Institution Press, 1991.

Barnes, Sandra, ed. *Africa's Ògún: Old World and New*. Bloomington: Indiana University Press, 1997.

Bascomb, William. *Ifá Divination: Communication between Gods and Men in West Africa*. Bloomington: Indiana University Press, 1969.

Bassey, Bassey Efiong. *Ékpè Efik: A Theosophical Perspective*. Victoria, BC: Trafford Publishing, 1998/2001.

Bastide, Roger. *African Civilizations in the New World*. New York: Harper and Row, 1971.

Bastide, Roger. *The African Religions of Brazil: Toward a Sociology of the Interpenetration of Civilizations*. Baltimore: Johns Hopkins University Press, [1960] 2007.

Beier, Ulli. "The Egúngún Cult." *Nigeria Magazine* 51 (1956): 380–92.

Brandon, George. *Santeria from Africa to the New World: The Dead Sell Memories*. Bloomington: Indiana University Press, 1997.

Brown, David H. *Santeria Enthroned: Art, Ritual, and Innovation in an Afro-Cuban Religion*. Chicago: University of Chicago Press, 2003.

Brown, Karen McCarthy. *Mama Lola: A Vodou Priestess in Brooklyn*. Los Angeles: University of California Press, 1991.

Cabrera, Lydia. *Anagó: Vocabulario Lucumí: El Yoruba Que Se Habla En Cuba*. La Habana: Ed. C.R., 1957.

Cabrera, Lydia, and Rosario Hiriart. *Yemayá y Ochún*. Miami: Ediciones Universal, [1980] 1996.

Cabrera, Lydia. *The Sacred Language of the Abakuá*. Translated by Ivor Miller and P. Gonzáles. Jackson: University Press of Mississippi, 2020.

Capone, Stefania. *Searching for Africa in Brazil: Power and Tradition in Candomblé*. Durham, NC: Duke University Press, 2010.

Caputo, Stela Guedes. "To Weave the Sacred Opá, the Temporary House of Death: To Know That the Father Teaches the Son in the Egún." Accessed June 1, 2018. https://www.scribd.com/document/74342578/entrevista-sobre-Egúngún.

Carvalho, José Jorge de, and Rita Segato. *Shango Cult in Recife, Brazil*. Caracas, Venezuela: Fundef, Conac, Oas, 1992.

Chambers Brothers. *Time Has Come Today*. LP, Columbia Records CS 9522, 1967.

Deren, Maya. *Divine Horsemen: The Voodoo Gods of Haiti*. New York: Vanguard Press, 1953.

Dos Santos, Juana Elbein. *Os Nàgôs e a Morte: Pàde, Àsèsè e o Culto Égun na Bahia*. Petropolis, Brazil: Editora Vozes, 2002.

Dos Santos, Juana Elbein, and Deoscoredes M. Dos Santos. "Ancestor Worship in Bahia." *Journal de la Societe des Americanistes* 58 (1969): 79–108.

Drewal, Henry. "The Arts of Egúngún among the Yorùbá Peoples." *African Arts* 11, no. 3 (April 1978): 18, 19, 97, 98.

Drewal, Henry. "Whirling Cloth, Breeze of Blessing: Egúngún Masquerades Among the Yorùbá." In *Homecomings, Crossings, and Passings: Life and Death in the African Diaspora*, edited by Regennia N. Williams, 175–206. Porter Ranch, CA: New World African Press, 2011.

Drewal, Henry John, and Margaret Thompson Drewal. *Gẹ̀lẹ̀dẹ́: Art and Female Power among the Yorùbá*. Bloomington: Indiana University Press, 1990.

Drewal, Henry John, and Margaret Thompson Drewal. "More Powerful Than Each Other: An Ẹ̀gbádò Classification of Egúngún." *African Arts* 11, no. 3 (April 1978): 28–39, 98.

Margaret Thompson Drewal. *Yorùbá Ritual: Performers, Play, Agency*. Bloomington: Indiana University Press, 1992.

Egúngún, Ancestralidade Africana no Brasil. Liner notes from the LP. SECNEB-Brazilian Society for Black Culture Studies, 1982.

Elẹ́buibọn, Ifayẹ́mí. *The Healing Power of Sacrifice*. New York: Athelia Henrietta Press, 2000.

Eltis, David. "The Diaspora of Yorùbá Speakers, 1650–1865: Dimensions and Implications." In *The Yorùbá Diaspora in the Atlantic World*, edited by Toyin Falola and Matt D. Childs, 17–39. Bloomington: Indiana University Press, 2004.

Eltis, David, and David Richardson. *Atlas of the Transatlantic Slave Trade*. New Haven: Yale University Press, 2010.

Fakayode, Fayemi Fatunde. *Iwure, Efficacious Prayer to Odù, the Supreme Force*. Ibadan, Nigeria: Ejiodi Home of Tradition, 2011.

Fakinlede, Kayode. *Beginner's Yorùbá*. New York: Hippocrene Books, 2005.

Falola, Toyin, and Matt D. Childs, eds. *The Yorùbá Diaspora in the Atlantic World*. Bloomington: Indiana University Press. 2004.

Favela Rising. Directed by Jeff Zimbalist and Matt Mochary. DVD. Side Track Films, 2005. http://www.favelarising.com.

Fitzgerald, Maryanne, Henry T. Drewal, and Moyo Ekedji. "Transformation Through Cloth: An Egúngún Costume of the Yorùbá." *African Arts* 28, no. 2 (Spring 1995): 54–57.

Galembo, Phyllis. *Divine Inspiration: Benin to Bahia*. New York: Athelia Henrietta Press, 1993.

Gleason, Judith. "Egúngún: The Return of the Ancestor in Masquerade Form Among the Yorùbá." Unpublished paper.

Gleason, Judith. *Ọya: In Praise of an African Goddess.* San Francisco: HarperCollins, 1987.

Hagedorn, Katherine J. *Divine Utterances: The Performance of Afro-Cuban Santería.* Washington DC: Smithsonian Books, 2001.

Houlberg, Marilyn Hammersley. "Egúngún Masquerades of the Remo Yorùbá." *African Arts* 11, no. 3 (April 1978a): 20–27, 100.

Houlberg, Marilyn Hammersley. "Notes on Egúngún Masquerades among the Ọ̀yọ́ Yorùbá." *African Arts* 11, no. 3 (April 1978): 56–61, 99.

Huston, Zora Heale. *Barracoon.* New York: Amistad/HarperCollins, 2018.

Ìdòwú, Bọ́láji E. *African Traditional Religion: A Definition.* Maryknoll, NY: Orbis Books, 1973.

Ìdòwú, Bọ́láji E. *Olódùmarè: God in Yorùbá Belief.* New York: Wazobia, [1962] 1994.

Kardec, Allen. *The Spirit's Book.* New York: Studium, 1980.

Landes, Ruth. *The City of Women.* Albuquerque: University of New Mexico Press, 1947.

Law, Robin. "Ethnicity and the Slave Trade: 'Lucumi' and 'Nago' as Ethnonyms in West Africa." *History of Africa* 24 (1997): 204–19.

Law, Robin. "The Evolution of the Brazilian Community in Ouidah." *Rethinking the African Diaspora: The Making of a Black Atlantic World in the Bight of Benin and Brazil,* edited by Kristin Mann and Edna G. Bay, 22–41. London: Frank Cass, 2001.

Lawal, Babatunde. *The Gẹ̀lẹ̀dẹ̀ Spectacle: Art, Gender, and Social Harmony in an African Culture.* Seattle: University of Washington Press, 1996.

Lawal, Babatunde. "The Living Dead: Art and Immortality Among the Yorùbá of Nigeria." *Africa: Journal of the International African Institute* 47, no. 1 (1977): 50–61.

Mann, Kristen and Edna G. Bay, eds. *Rethinking the African Diaspora: The Making of a Black Atlantic World in the Bight of Benin and Brazil.* London: Frank Cass, 2001.

Mariano, Agnes. *Obaràyí.* Salvador, Brazil: Barabô, 2009.

Mason, Michael Atwood. *Living Santeria: Rituals and Experiences in an Afro-Cuban Religion.* Washington, DC: Smithsonian Books, 2002.

Matory, J. Lorand. *Black Atlantic Religion: Tradition, Transnationalism, and Matriarchy in the Afro-Brazilian Candomblé.* Princeton, NJ: Princeton University Press, 2005.

Morton-Williams, Peter. "Yorùbá Responses to the Fear of Death." *Africa: Journal of the International African Institute* 30, no. 1 (January 1960): 34–40.

Murphy, Joseph. *Santería: African Spirits in America.* Boston: Beacon Press, [1988] 1993.

Murphy, Joseph. *Working the Spirit: Ceremonies of the African Diaspora.* Boston: Beacon Press, 1994.

Murphy, Joseph, and Mei-Mei Sanford, eds. *Ọṣun across the Waters: A Yorùbá Goddess in Africa and the Americas.* Bloomington: Indiana University Press, 2001.

Ogunbile, David O. "Ẹ́rìndínlógún: The Seeing Eyes of Sacred Shells and Stones." In *Ọṣun across the Water: A Yorùbá Goddess in Africa and the Americas.* edited by Joseph M. Murphy and Mei-Mei Sanford, 189–212. Bloomington: Indiana University Press, 2001.

Olajubu, Oludare. "The Yorùbá Egúngún Masquerade Cult and Its Role in the Society." In *The Masquerade in Nigerian History and Culture*, edited by Nwanna Nzewunwa, 389–409. Port Harcourt, Nigeria: University of Port Harcourt Press, 1983.

Olajubu, Oludare, and J. R. O. Ojo. "Some Aspects of Ọ̀yọ́ Yorùbá Masquerades." *Africa: Journal of the International African Institute* 47, no. 3 (1977): 253–75.

Olmstead, David. "Comparative Notes on Yorùbá and Lucumí." *Language* 29: 157–64.

Ológundúdú, Adédayò. *The Cradle of Yorùbá Culture.* New York: Institute of Yorùbá Culture, 2008.

Omari-Tunkara, Mikelle Smith. *Manipulating the Sacred: Yorùbá Art, Ritual, and Resistance in Brazilian Candomblé.* Detroit, MI: Wayne State University Press, 2005.

Omari-Tunkara, Mikelle Smith. "The Role of the Gods in Afro-Brazilian Ancestral Ritual." *African Arts* 23, no. 1 (1989): 54–61, 103.

Otero, Solimar. *Afro-Cuban Diasporas in the Atlantic World.* Rochester, NY: Boydell and Brewer, 2010.

Parés, Luis Nicolau. "Nagoization in Bahian Candomblé." In *The Yorùbá Diaspora in the Atlantic World*, edited by Toyin Falola and Matt D. Childs, 185–208. Bloomington: Indiana University Press, 2004.

Pemberton, John. "Egúngún Masquerades of the Igbomina People." *African Arts* 11, no. 3 (April 1978): 40–47, 99, 100.

Pessoa de Castro, Yeda. "Religions of African Origin in Brazil: Designations, origins and new and little-known cults. Proceedings of the meeting of experts on the Survival of African Religious Traditions in the Caribbean and Latin America." San Luis de Maranhao, Brazil, June 1985.

Pierre Verger: Mensageiro Entre Dois Mundos (Messenger Between Two Worlds). Directed by Lula Buarque de Hollanda. DVD. Europa Filmes, 1996.

Reis, João José, and Beatriz Galotti Mamigonian. "Nago and Mina: The Yorùbá Diaspora in Brazil." In *The Yorùbá Diaspora in the Atlantic*

World, edited by Toyin Falola and Matt D. Childs, 77–110. Blooming-ton: Indiana University Press, 2004.

Roberts, Katy. *Live at L'Archipel.* CD. Independent release, 2005.

Rush, Dana. *Vodun in Coastal Bénin: Unfinished, Open-Ended, Global.* Nashville, TN: Vanderbilt University Press, 2013.

Schiltz, Marc. "Egúngún Masquerades in Iganna." *African Arts* 11, no. 3 (1978): 48–55, 100.

Simpson, George Eaton. *Yorùbá Religion and Medicine in Ibadan.* Ibadan, Nigeria: Ibadan University Press, 1980.

Smith, Robert. "The Alafin in Exile: A Study of the Igboho Period in Ọ̀yọ́ History." *Journal of African History* 6, no. 1 (1965): 57–77.

Suzuki, Shunryo. *Zen Mind, Beginner's Mind.* New York: Weatherhill, 1995.

Taylor, Cecil. *Silent Tongues.* Arista Records, 1975.

Thompson, Robert Farris. *African Art in Motion.* Los Angeles: University of California Press, 1974.

Thompson, Robert Farris. *Face of the Gods: Art and Altars of Africa and the African Americas.* New York: Museum for African Art, 1993.

Thompson, Robert Farris. *Flash of the Spirit: African and Afro-American Art and Philosophy.* New York: Vintage Books, 1983.

Thompson, Robert Farris. "Lecture on *Daughters of the Dust.*" 2006. Accessed April 21, 2020. https://www.youtube.com/watch?v=b30HaCi5fq4.

Thompson, Robert Farris. "The Three Warriors: Atlantic Altars of Èṣù, Ògún, and Ọ̀ṣọọsi." In *The Yorùbá Artist: New Theoretical Perspec-tives on African Arts,* edited by Rowland Abiodun, Henry J. Drewal, and John Pemberton III, 225–39. Washington, DC: Smithsonian Institu-tion Press, 1994.

Thompson, Robert Farris, and Joseph Cornet. *Four Moments of the Sun: Kongo Art in Two Worlds.* Washington: National Gallery of Art, 1981.

Verger, Pierre. *Ewé: The Use of Plants in Yorùbá Society.* São Paulo: Edi-tora Schwartz, [1967] 1995.

Verger, Pierre. *Notícias da Bahia: 1850.* Salvador, Brazil.

Verger, Pierre. "The Rise and Fall of the Worship of Ìyàmi Òṣòròngà Among the Yorùbá." In *Pierre Fatumbi Verger Articles, Vol. I,* trans-lated by Christophe Brunski, 37–196. New Jersey: Black Madonna Enterprises, [1965] 2007.

Voeks, Robert A. *Sacred Leaves of Candomblé: African Magic, Medicine, and Religion in Brazil.* Austin: University of Texas Press, 1997.

Wafer, James William. *The Taste of Blood: Spirit Possession in Brazilian Candomblé.* Philadelphia: University of Pennsylvania Press, 1991.

Warner-Lewis, Maureen. *Yoruba Songs of Trinidad*. London: Karnak
    House, 1984.
Warner-Lewis, Maureen. *Trinidad Yoruba: From Mother-Tongue to
    Memory*. Tuscaloosa: University of Alabama Press, 1996.
Williams, Regennia N., ed. *Homecomings, Crossings, and Passings: Life
    and Death in the African Diaspora*. Porter Ranch, CA: New World
    African Press, 2011.
Wolff, Norma H. "Egúngún Costuming in Abeokuta." *African Arts* 15, no.
    3 (May 1982): 66–70, 91.

INDEX

ABOUT THE AUTHOR

Brian Willson is a *babaláwo* (specialist in the Yorùbá system of Ifá) and a senior member of temple Ilé Ọ̀kànràn Onílẹ̀ based in Ibadan and New York. He has been a practitioner of African diasporic religious practices for over forty years. He received his DMA from City University of New York Graduate Center, has lectured or performed in over twenty-five countries, and is a trustee on the board of Education Africa.

CPSIA information can be obtained
at www.ICGtesting.com
Printed in the USA
BVHW090507270621
609933BV00002B/4